THE DEADLY GAMBLE

A Post-Mortem of the

World Trade Center Collapse

RICHARD E. KLEIN, PhD

DUMB
DICKIE
PRESS.™

Published by Dumb Dickie Press

ISBN-13: 978-1-0921-3362-3
ISBN-10: 1-0921-3362-3

Cover design by Ellen Meyer and Vicki Lesage

Disclaimer

The author, Richard E. Klein, is not licensed as a Professional Engineer, is not trained or qualified in law, has no training or expertise in matters related to building codes and fire safety standards of buildings, has never provided consulting services related to engineering of structures, and has never accepted remuneration for professional services rendered as per engineering and design of structures and legal matters. This document has not been subjected to peer review. The opinions expressed are those of the author and should not be relied upon until and unless verified by independent and reliable sources. Persons with need of counsel in matters pertaining to engineering, building construction codes, fire safety standards, public safety, and/or law are advised to seek qualified licensed professionals and/or counsel.

"The requirement for heat-insulating protection on tall, steel-framed building structural beams is an absolute must. I would never, under any circumstances, approve, under fire safety codes, any tall structure that lacked such protection."

~Frank C. Schaper, Retired Deputy Fire Chief, St. Louis, Missouri

Table of Contents

Preface

In pondering the outcome and circumstances of 9/11, a horrific day in America's history, some obvious and inevitable questions arise in my engineering-driven mind:

What if proper heat insulation had been in place on steel structural members as per New York City and accepted building code standards? To be more specific, would the outcome have been changed? Said yet another way, would lives have been saved? Also, would the collapses of the two towers have been averted?

This book tells my personal story about my decades-long interactions with members of the civil engineering profession. My encounter with the World Trade Center (1973-2001) took place in 1975, over twenty-five years prior to its collapse on September 11, 2001. During this visit, I sensed that matters pertaining to fire safety standards and building codes were not in conformity with accepted practices. I raised my concerns with the responsible authorities: the World Trade Center's structural engineers. I was informed that a decision had been made to seek and accept a building code waiver thereby exempting the application of heat insulation protection on the World Trade Center's steel structural beams.

In this work, I explain why professional canons of ethics precluded me from making any form of public statement as to the risks associated with the World Trade Center and the fire safety code waiver.

My aim in writing this is to establish and document two central points: The first is my credibility as a witness. To that let me add the adjective *expert* onto the word witness. Despite my many shortcomings, I was amply qualified to grasp the significance of the role of heat-protective insulation practices in steel-framed tall structures.

The second—and I've included substantial background detail to support this—is the fact that the World Trade Center stood as a menace in downtown Manhattan that was poised to fail upon provocation.

To boil down my story to the basics, my testimony is simple. I testify that the World Trade Center, as of December 23, 1975, lacked thermal insulation protection on its steel structural framing. I personally saw naked, unprotected steel structural members in the South Tower at the

82nd floor. I was told by Mr. Fred Chang, Professional Engineer (PE), that thermal insulation foam was in place only on lower floors, from the ground level up to the 20th floor.

Numerous studies and reports on the September 11, 2001 collapse abound. Many suggest that asbestos-based insulation application was halted in 1970 as the WTC construction progressed. Many imply that an alternate thermal insulation was then applied.

My eyewitness testimony stands in stark contrast. The matter, in my view, was not a question of substandard insulation, or if the insulation in the impact zones became dislodged. I assert that there was no insulation protection at all on the steel structural members.

I wish to recount a story from my days in Boy Scouts. Yes, I was an Eagle Scout. What I say is said with the phrase in mind, "On my Scout's Honor."

From left: Richard E. Klein and brothers Donald and Frederick

I joined Boy Scout Troop 202 in the spring of 1950. The troop was sponsored by the Wilcoxson School PTA in Stratford, Connecticut. I took to Scouting, advancing in rank and becoming confident with camping. With camping came meal preparation and outdoor cooking. I took note of an advertisement. "No soggy under-crust" proclaimed the advertisement for Morton's Chicken Pot Pie. I purchased one, and took it camping. In my altruistic mind, I anticipated a chicken pot pie with a crisp and tasty under-crust. To my astonishment, I discovered that my chicken pot pie had no under-crust at all. Without an under-crust, it certainly wasn't soggy.

I assert that the WTC didn't have soggy or defective structural insulation, but rather the WTC had no insulation at all. You can take that on my Scout's Honor.

Introduction

Within our national heritage and history, several great tragedies stand out. I will mention four: (1) the Great Chicago Fire that started on October 8, 1871 and continued for several days; (2) the Johnstown Flood of 1889; (3) the sinking of the *Titanic* in 1912; and (4) the collapse of the World Trade Center Twin Towers (WTC) on September 11, 2001. All four tragedies shared commonalities. All involved the shortcomings of things that were man-made. All came as a surprise at the time, but all embodied serious errors when viewed in hindsight.

The Great Chicago Fire was triggered by a cow kicking over a lantern, but humans had set the stage. The stage was merely vast numbers of wooden structures in close proximity. Few people envisioned such an enormous fire. Firefighters discovered that adjacent firefighting companies couldn't interconnect their hoses. National firefighting standards were unheard of at the time.

The Johnstown Flood happened because an earthen dam, some fourteen miles upriver from Johnstown, Pennsylvania, failed, resulting in the deaths of over 2,000 people.

The *Titanic* failed for numerous reasons. The loss of life was needless. Arrogance in design caused the elimination of adequate numbers of lifeboats. After all, the *Titanic* was cutting edge so lifeboats were deemed unnecessary.

The WTC was constructed by a self-important closed club of pseudo-experts. Arrogance ruled the day, as a decision was made that heat-insulating foam protection of the steel support columns was unnecessary and thereby eliminated. The decision to stop the application of spray-on foam had two roots. First, environmental concerns had heightened about the hazards of asbestos. Second, wind-induced sway necessitated that work stop pending the installation of 10,000 viscous-elastic dampers in each tower. Any delay in occupancy would impact the ability to generate rental income. An unoccupied building doesn't generate rental income.

Considering these four tragedies, the commonalities increasingly become clear in retrospect: arrogance, conceit, stupidity, and hubris. All four tragedies took the lives of innocent victims.

When massive building projects are undertaken, they require the coordinated effort of many people and resources. Society has created a thing called government. One purpose of government is to oversee the welfare of the public good. The governmental overseers failed in all four of the above cited tragedies. If proper oversight had been in place, the four respective disasters would have been averted.

What made the WTC disaster different was that government itself had key roles in the World Trade Center disaster:

- The WTC was the brainchild of a powerful and unique governmental entity—the Port Authority of New York and New Jersey (PANYNJ). The PANYNJ financed, built, owned, and managed the WTC Twin Towers.
- The Port Authority served as its own overseer. For example, the WTC was exempt from New York City building codes.
- The hijacked airliners were subject to Transportation Security Administration (TSA) screening of passengers. The policies and practices of the TSA obviously failed. Passengers who could have otherwise intervened were disarmed, rendered impotent, and under behavioral protocols to remain passive and certainly nonconfrontational.
- WTC management policies dictated that the occupants of the WTC remain at their work locations. Evacuation of occupants from the Twin Towers on 9/11 was met with Port Authority resistance.

In this book, I argue that the World Trade Center collapse represented the most grievous of the four cited tragedies. Yes, terrorists commandeered four airliners on 9/11, but few know—until now—that the collapse was a certainty because the World Trade Center was constructed based on shortcuts. The structural engineers made a fateful and willful choice to waive the inclusion of heat-insulating foam in most portions of the WTC Twin Towers. With no heat-insulating foam in the upper floors, fuel from the hijacked airliners quickly elevated the temperature of the supporting structural steel beams. Sadly, in post-collapse testimony, responsible parties made misleading and false statements as to the construction standards.

Both the *Titanic* and the WTC were designed by highly trained and certified experts. History now makes one point clear—the experts came up short. The emperor was wearing no clothes. Many are familiar with the sinking of the *Titanic* on April 15, 1912. The design of the ship incorporated sixteen supposedly watertight compartments. In fact, the compartments were only watertight so long as the *Titanic* stayed close to level.

The design was predicated on a probability argument. It was beyond all reasoning that an incident would simultaneously involve more than four of the compartments. As such, the *Titanic* was promoted in its pre-sailing days as being unsinkable.

Given this mindset, the designers viewed an adequate number of lifeboats as extraneous, unnecessary, and unfashionable as they wanted to keep the decks of the *Titanic* clear of such unsightly safeguards. After all, it was a state-of-the-art luxury liner. Their focus was on the social life, the gourmet food, the finery of the table settings, the music, the ballroom, and the vessel's advanced speed. A voyage aboard the *Titanic* was more than crossing the ocean. It was a way for the pompous, wealthy, and elites to hobnob.

Yet after hitting an iceberg that flooded six compartments, the *Titanic* ultimately proved to be sinkable. History records that the ship's captain, Edward John Smith, went down with the ship. J. Bruce Ismay, the managing director of the White Star Line, was the highest-ranking official to survive and was the target of much public scorn for escaping ahead of women and children.

With this overview of the four cited needless human tragedies, I am now prepared to embark upon my personal story—the story of my involvement with civil engineers in general and with the particular structural engineers responsible for the construction details of the World Trade Center.

Following World War II and into the 1960s, the principles and practices of feedback control systems became an important part of engineering educational curricula. This was especially true in both electrical and mechanical engineering. My studies regarding feedback control systems as a graduate student at Purdue University in the 1960s had been cutting-edge, classified, and even secret during WWII.

In my mind, being a practitioner of feedback control systems was like residing within a black hole. I use the metaphor black hole because:

- When standing from afar and looking in, there is nothing for the outsider to see.
- The subject matter of feedback control systems isn't physical, but rather symbolic and even illusionary. It certainly isn't something tangible such as poured concrete reinforced with steel framing.
- Those within the black hole speak an entirely different language compared to those outside. To the outsider, the language is seemingly pure gibberish.

As such, those standing outside of feedback control systems might look in, but they see nothing. To them, if they see nothing, it is logical that nothing is there. The situation is analogous to looking into a black hole.

The story of my involvement with tall structures had its origins in the early 1970s. With my background in mechanical engineering and systems control principles, I endeavored to apply feedback systems theory to civil engineering structures. My goal was to mitigate unwanted wind-induced sway in tall structures. My activities were purely academic, thus expressed as ideas on paper. What I did was conjectural and hypothetical. I lacked access to a tall structure. I had scant chance to ever try out my ideas on a real-world physical building.

In hindsight, it was foolish of me to remain focused on one professional belief and for so long—believing that I could enter and impact a world dominated by architects, big-time investors, and civil engineers. After devoting decades to this endeavor, I ended up with little to show for my time and efforts.

The story of that forty-plus years of struggle was embodied in the events of one fateful day—December 23, 1975. I will now tell that story, albeit in abbreviated form. My decades of detailed work and background will be recounted in a more comprehensive version in subsequent chapters.

Part 1 – My Encounter with the World Trade Center

My Landmark Research Paper

My research into stabilization of tall structures started in the early 1970s. After enlisting two colleagues, Dr. Cristino Cusano and Dr. James J. Stukel, we jointly researched, submitted, and presented what became a landmark paper. The paper's title was "Investigation of a Method to Stabilize Wind Induced Oscillations in Large Structures." [1] The paper was presented at the 1972 ASME (American Society of Mechanical Engineers) Winter Annual Meeting in New York City.

Dickie (Richard E.) Klein as a young professor

The 1972 ASME paper on tall building stabilization suggested using feedback control system theoretic principles. In the four decades since publication, the Klein, Cusano, and Stukel paper has received considerable recognition. Numerous authorities recognized that paper as the start of research into structural stabilization using feedback control system principles. This general topic has subsequently matured, as entire symposia and journals now address what are called smart materials and intelligent structures.

Although few persons have ever read the Klein, Cusano, and Stukel 1972 paper [1], the number of authorities who have cited that paper now must be several hundred or more. In my worldview, a scholarly paper that is cited perhaps five or ten times represents a big deal for many authors. A paper that gets cited, say, thirty times, is awesome. In academic circles, a paper that gets cited hundreds of times, as is the case with my 1972 ASME paper, represents what can truly be called a landmark.

In the photograph above, the author is holding a copy of the 1972 ASME paper.

In 1975, the structural engineers for the World Trade Center (WTC) encountered wind-induced sway issues. My 1972 ASME paper had come to their attention. They contacted me regarding the sway issues and possible retrofit remedies. Based on an invitation, I traveled to New York City to meet with the structural engineers responsible for the World Trade Center.

My Visit to the World Trade Center

The World Trade Center Twin Towers had sway issues, but the reason for my visit was sway of a smaller adjacent building. That smaller building, smaller comparatively, was referred to simply as 22 Cortlandt Street. After my consultation there, I requested a tour of the South Tower. Some of its upper floors were still undergoing construction, and the interiors had not yet been closed off so I was able to view the structural support columns and ceiling trusses.

During my eye-witness inspection tour, I noted a serious defect or building code issue. The defect was unrelated to the initial sway problem, but my eyes saw construction practices that didn't add up. A decision had been made during construction of the WTC to dispense with the requirement to protect the steel structural support columns and overhead trusses with heat-insulating material. In my estimation, this constituted a serious design and construction flaw.

As my account continues, I need to explain that the statements and assertions which follow are speculative to some extent. My comments are based on the best evidence available to me. In a sense, I have strived to connect the dots that emerged within an otherwise hazy picture, attempting to make sense of a murky collection of facts. The picture is muddled for varied reasons:

1. Most original drawings and construction records for the WTC were stored in offices within the WTC—and thus were destroyed in the 9/11 collapse. Records stored elsewhere weren't electronic, but rather on paper stored in musty and forgotten boxes. Recycling has claimed many. Other records were simply lost. Extant records of the WTC are few.

2. The WTC was a project conceived by, financed, built, and operated by a powerful and unique institution—the Port Authority of New York and New Jersey. The PANYNJ was an

empire unto itself. Its origins stemmed from a culture in New York City created in large by Robert Moses (1888-1981) [2]. By the time the WTC was being built, Robert Moses was aged and waning in power, but his hand was still there in the DNA of the PANYNJ. Few people, even U.S. Presidents, could challenge and stand up against Robert Moses. The Port Authority was a mixture of government and private ownership, largely immune from oversight. The PANYNJ was its own watchdog.

3. The PANYNJ kept its records and documentation locked away from outside scrutiny.

4. Owners and investors in tall buildings commonly prohibit the monitoring of building sway. No law requires that a building's sway be measured, which is typically done by accelerometer recordings. If accelerations aren't measured, then the recordings can't be subject to discovery. I use the word discovery in its legal context.

5. Because of continued threats of terrorism following 9/11, responsible officials were and still are under pressure to keep secret varied specifics of the WTC's design and construction. In my own circumstance, I remained silent for decades. I was hesitant to tell terrorists details of our societal infrastructure and its vulnerabilities.

6. It is the very nature of the construction industry, especially as related to cutting-edge structures, to maintain internal design and construction details as proprietary.

7. An old adage states one reality well: Victory has a hundred fathers, but defeat is but an orphan. The point is that the WTC collapse debacle represented a defeat of immense proportions. The persons responsible for the design and construction decisions tended to seek a position deep in the shadows. It became easy to blame nineteen terrorists and to not point out how construction shortcuts created a dangerous and precipitous situation.

8. Half a century has passed since the WTC was designed and constructed. It is reasonable to believe that many persons who made design and construction decisions in the late 1960s are now either deceased or elderly at best. The passage of time has dimmed the light of culpability.

9. Few persons predicted 9/11, so therefore saw no need to keep old records. In my own situation, when I retired in 1998, I disposed of most of my files related to tall structures and my

research on structures. I was turning to a new chapter in my life. But then 9/11 happened.

With that disclaimer stated, here is how I have connected the WTC dots.

The original WTC architectural specifications surely called for heat-insulating material on the supporting steel beams and trusses, but three factors cropped up. In writing this story, I refer to the first, second, and third, but the ordering of the three factors is not established. My usage of first, second, and third reflects only the order of my discussion of each.

1. The first factor had its roots in environmental asbestos standards, as asbestos-based insulation was becoming an identified and/or perceived hazard. Early in 1970, asbestos-based insulation was being applied on the lower floors of the North Tower. Air quality concerns prompted a stoppage.

2. The second factor was that although alternative insulating materials existed, the certification and testing of the alternatives was in its infancy. The option to switch to alternatives was not a trivial undertaking. In my view, alternatives to asbestos-based insulation were available, but were not as well-tested and documented as compared to asbestos-based insulation.

3. Because of the need to mitigate unwanted wind-induced swaying in the twin towers, a retrofit remedy called for installing dampers. The installation of the dampers was best accomplished if insulating foam was not present. The requirement to modify the steel framing therefore prompted a cessation in the application of heat-insulating material on the structural beams and trusses.

I will now expound on this third factor, which has not previously been reported on to any significant extent.

The twin structures were framed out and their exteriors clad in the late 1960s. Following external completion, the twin towers exhibited unexpected and unwanted aerodynamic-induced swaying. A retrofit remedy was then proposed. This solution was suggested by the late Dr. Alan G. Davenport, formerly the director of the Boundary Layer Wind Tunnel at the University of Western Ontario. The 3M Company designed and manufactured 20,000 viscous-elastic dampers, 10,000 to be retrofit-installed in each tower. The objective was to increase the structural damping by dissipating unwanted sway energy.

The damper installation retrofit necessitated a stoppage or change of other work. The dampers had to be put into place. Dampers were to be installed by attaching them to overhead truss ends on all floors above the 10th. The attachment procedure required some welding—welding that would be significantly easier if the structural beams were not insulation covered.

Delays and retrofits in any construction project are always costly. One expedient and cost-saving solution was to forgo the application of heat-protective insulation.

During my inspection tour and consultation on December 23, 1975, I observed structural beams devoid of the customary code-mandated heat insulation. Moreover, it was obvious to me that other work was in progress; work never done if the spray-on of insulating foam was yet to occur. The interior areas were being finished out. The step of application of insulation had been eliminated from the work schedule. It was clear that a purposeful decision had been made to forgo the application of heat-insulating material on the load-bearing structural steel beams. In my estimation, this shortcut placed the structure, the occupants, and the city-at-large at undue risk.

I raised my concerns with my hosts, the WTC's structural engineers. I directed my concerns to Fred Chang, Professional Engineer. I was told that a building code waiver had been requested and had been granted.

As we stood together looking directly at exposed structural beams and ceiling trusses, Chang was emphatic. He stated that the absence of heat-insulating foam or insulation was based on a code waiver.

Mr. Chang proceeded to list five reasons for the waiver. As a professor and technical speaker, I took note of these five justifications, which were foundational to the request for and the granting of the structural code waiver. In my mind, any speaker who states the number five and then outlines the five reasons has already planned the subject matter in anticipation of a possible challenge. The reasons were as follows:

1. The tower interiors were outfitted with ceiling-mounted heat-activated sprinklers.
2. The towers had provision for early detection of fire, including sprinkler water flow monitored according to zone.
3. The towers, upon occupancy, would have few combustible materials within.
4. Any fire outbreak would be localized.
5. Firefighting crews would respond quickly, thereby containing any outbreak of fire.

Chang went on to summarize his position. The World Trade Center represented a new standard and new technology in building design and construction. He stated that heat-insulating protective foam was no longer necessary and implied that construction techniques and rules were radically altered. Past practices were no longer applicable. The new rules and methods significantly lowered construction costs on a square-footage basis. Obviously, the structural engineers and many others assumed the twin towers to be cutting edge and indestructible, just like the designers of the unsinkable *Titanic*.

The entire scheme for the design and building of the World Trade Center boiled down to the matter of minimizing the cost of construction per square foot of rentable floor space. Chang then even stated the dollar cost for construction per square foot.

Mr. Chang returned to his primary statement. Heat insulation covering the steel framing was no longer necessary according to the new standards. The world had entered a new era of high-rise construction guidelines and standards—or so I was told.

The persons making these assertions were licensed Professional Engineers. I lacked such credentials. My engineering specialization was in control systems. California at the time was the only state that licensed control systems engineers. I did not practice or live in California.

I was also bound by the ASME Code of Ethics, as published by the American Society of Mechanical Engineers (ASME). As a professor teaching mechanical engineering and a member of ASME, I was bound by, morally obligated to follow, and would be judged accordingly by the ASME Code of Ethics. That Code of Ethics placed restrictions on my ability to tell the world one thing—that the World Trade Center Twin Towers, as constructed, constituted a flagrant public safety menace. In my estimation, the WTC Twin Towers embodied an obvious fire and death trap and were poised to collapse given provocation. That provocation came on September 11, 2001.

At this point I will elaborate on how my actions were restricted by the ASME Code of Ethics. One code mandated that mechanical engineers should only perform services in their field or fields of expertise. The phraseology was based, in my estimation, on the presumption of specialization. While I was schooled and trained in mechanical engineering, I was a generalist rather than a specialist. In my view, I was excluded from performing mechanical engineering services, at least in projects involving public safety. In this book and elsewhere, I argue that mechanical engineering is an art. The true mechanical engineer is a generalist skilled in the art of mechanical engineering. In contrast, the ASME Code of Ethics was written based on the presumption of specialization.

Moreover, my conscience dictated that I follow the Code of Ethics. My upbringing had conditioned me to behave properly. Upon sensing a problem involving public safety, I directed my concerns face-to-face to the responsible WTC structural engineers.

A second code prohibited mechanical engineers from making public statements unless they could do so objectively. As pertaining to civil engineering structures, I had investigated feedback applications to achieve sway stabilization and mitigation, but my objectivity had been challenged by numerous persons. Even my colleagues in mechanical engineering made jokes about "Klein blinds" perched on top of buildings. Objectivity is an abstract concept. The determination as to what is objective had been made subject to a vote.

I was in a distant minority. There was no signal to fight and to pursue one's dream. The ASME Code of Ethics was structured to protect a conservative profession. Numerous licensed Professional Engineers had deemed that heat insulation on WTC structural beams could be waived.

Mechanical Engineering, a Regulated Profession

It is appropriate to elaborate on mechanical engineering as a profession. The ASME Code of Ethics was founded on certain unstated principles:

- Engineering is viewed by many as a science as opposed to an art form. Only those persons trained in the sciences are qualified to perform engineering services.
- Engineering is a reserved term, a word protected by law.
- Only those who have passed examinations and have met other qualifications can call themselves engineers, or more appropriately Professional Engineers.

The foundations on which mechanical engineering was built excluded the non-qualified. Too many early steam engine pressure vessels blew apart, so standards were created. Pressure vessels became subject to regulation. As regulations and standards evolved, mechanical engineering evolved as a licensed profession.

I submit that engineering, in the broader sense, is an art form. Creativity is central. The goal is for the betterment of society by making the world a better place. Electric starters, automatic transmissions, and refrigeration are but a few examples of engineering achievements. The list of creations that have helped achieve a better life has no end. It is absurd to suggest that creativity is some exclusive protected right.

For the duration of my tenure as a faculty member teaching mechanical engineering, my focus was on getting my students to think creatively. For obvious reasons, I didn't fit into the proper mold. At the University of Illinois, even the name of the department was changed to reflect the emphasis on science. The role of creativity has been brushed aside. The name selected was Department of Mechanical Sciences and Engineering.

Other professional areas have avoided licensing by government. One notable example is Information Technology (IT). Consequently, IT has leap-frogged way past traditional regulated professions. The advances being made in IT are mind-boggling. Traditional regulated professions such as mechanical engineering and civil engineering are moving at a snail's pace in comparison.

An added note is that renaissance persons are not welcome in traditional engineering professions, yet free spirits are enjoying a heyday in IT fields. My millennial grandson Noah has no interest in more academic degrees. He sees rather that success is determined by accomplishments—things created and generated into being by creative thinking.

PANYNJ Granted Itself a Waiver

The matter of ownership of the World Trade Center sheds considerable light on the collapse. The WTC was planned by, financed, built, and operated by the Port Authority of New York and New Jersey (PANYNJ). As such, the WTC was a governmental undertaking and project.

I speculate that the City of New York did not have the final say in matters such as building codes and fire safety standards. In my opinion, the Port Authority of New York and New Jersey merely asked itself for a code waiver. The code waiver was then granted.

I will go so far as to also suggest that the New York City's Fire Department crews were obligated by prior agreement to respond, as they did on 9/11—but the City of New York fire inspectors lacked jurisdiction. I have no validation, so my statement stands as unsupported speculation on my part.

I want to come back to my role as an invited outside consultant and observer. As a disclaimer, I was not a licensed Professional Engineer. In contrast, my hosts were licensed PEs, and thus qualified by law to sign off on structural designs and construction practices. My area of expertise was in mathematics of systems theory, quite afar from structures and civil engineering. By training, engineers in general are disciplined and get-along people. Engineers are expected to act civilly and to respect other engineers. Traditions dictate how things are done and have been done in the past.

On December 23, 1975, I had raised my concerns in a professional manner about the absence of heat insulation material on the WTC structural support beams and overhead trusses. I directed my concerns to the responsible persons—the WTC structural engineers. I was given answers by licensed and qualified civil engineers and I was professionally obligated to accept those answers.

The ASME Code of Ethics also required that I make no public statements unless I could do so objectively. By that time in 1975, my objectivity had been challenged. The challenges were rooted in written negative blind reviews of my research papers. Some of these reviews attacked my qualifications as well as my objectivity. Reviewers said things such as:

- Klein is not familiar with the literature.
- Klein is bitter because his ideas have not been accepted.
- Klein's work is pointless. The damping problem in tall structures has already been solved.

The editors of professional publications used these types of reviews as justification for rejecting my submitted manuscripts and research proposals. In general, my ideas were not contested, but rather my qualifications and my lack of objectivity were cited.

In regard to the WTC safety aspects, I felt professionally obligated to refrain from issuing any public statement. Options such as a letter to the editor and picketing in front of the WTC were not available to me.

On September 11, 2001, more than 2,700 people perished in the collapse of the World Trade Center Twin Towers. The death toll included 343 NYC fire fighters and 71 law enforcement police who had responded. The collapse was, in my view, a certainty given the provocation caused by the two fuel-laden airliners deliberately impacting the WTC twin structures.

No Thermal Protection on Structural Members

As a disclaimer, I never saw or asked to see any written documentation of the building code waiver, but instead took Mr. Chang at his word. We were at the time on-site in a walking tour, and not in his office. No documentation was at hand, and I never questioned the validity of Chang's statements.

What I saw and was told that day hit me like a ton of bricks. It was incredulous to think that the building codes applicable to the WTC had been somehow relaxed. It was also incredulous to imagine that fire safety inspectors would have signed off on a "no foam required" waiver.

My primary thrust herein is to state emphatically that on December 23, 1975, no protective insulating foam or material was present on the structural beams that I inspected. Moreover, according to Mr. Chang, no insulating foam was in place from the 21st floor and up.

Of course, the presence or absence of heat-protective insulating material has been discussed elsewhere in various WTC post-collapse reports and studies. Some pundits claimed that the impacting airliners tore away the protective insulation. Such claims are false, misguided, and inherently self-serving for the benefit of those making the claims.

The WTC lead structural designer, Mr. Leslie E. Robertson, PE, stated in post-collapse documentation that the WTC building's architectural design and construction met all applicable standards, clearly implying that heat-protective insulation was present. I strongly disagree with Mr. Robertson's statements. The World Trade Center structural beams had no protective insulation. According to Mr. Chang, as told to me on December 23, 1975, only the lower twenty stories had insulation protection. The hijackers didn't aim that low.

It can be argued that in making his statement Mr. Robertson was seeking some greater benefit to our society, such that enemies of America would not be informed of our infrastructure's weaknesses. My sense is that the facts regarding the 9/11 collapse need to be made public.

Large portions of the WTC structures collapsed mechanically, as opposed to being consumed by fire. The intense fires in each tower were localized, confined to the floors impacted by the terrorist-controlled airliners. Excessive heat combined with an absence of spray-on insulating foam caused critical structural members to fail. Overheated steel loses its structural properties. Critical steel beams in the WTC Twin Towers, upon failing, started the collapse mechanism. The vast aggregate of the towers failed because the progressive collapse had started.

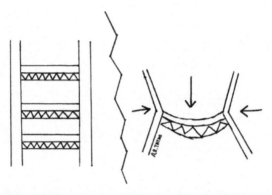

As depicted above, the simplified sketch on the left shows the prefabricated ceiling trusses supporting the concrete floors. Upon reaching and/or exceeding the critical failure temperature, the ceiling trusses failed. As depicted in the right sketch, gravity caused the respective concrete-supported floor to sag. The sagging caused the respective ends of the affected concrete floor(s) and trusses to exert inward loads on the vertical columns.

In addition, the many 3M dampers caused the sagging floors and ceiling trusses to apply bending moments on the respective vertical support columns. The ceiling trusses were originally designed to be connected to the vertical support beams with pinned connections. Pinned connections, by design, don't support a moment beyond the Coulomb (or dry) friction in the joints. Because the 3M dampers had been retrofitted onto all truss ends in the impacted zones, the failure of the overhead trusses when heated caused significant bending moments to be applied to the vertical support columns. The massive weight of the sagging concrete floor(s) overloaded the truss-end connections. As an analogy, the weakened but protruding truss-end attachments acted like prybars. Prybars have two points of contact. The original pinned joint pulled the vertical column(s) inward. A short distance below, the 3M damper in compression acted as the prybar's fulcrum, thus pushing outward. The combination of the two forces, forces in opposing directions (referred to in mechanics as a couple), applied immense bending moments to the vertical columns. The extended long lever-arm amplified the bending moment. The vertical support columns were not designed to carry and withstand those added bending moments.

Because the collapse of each tower was initiated by the failures of the overhead trusses, the retrofitting of the 3M dampers materially altered and exacerbated the progressive collapses.

Because the overhead blocks of floors fell straight down, it is plausible that the vertical columns failed simultaneously. I assert that the vertical columns failed mechanically, caused by buckling.

Moreover, the buckling of the vertical columns resulted from the applied moment and the inward pull caused by the sagging floor(s). The bending moments were created by the presence of the retrofitted 3M dampers.

Heating caused the failure of the ceiling trusses. Heat did not cause the failure of the vertical columns. I reject any argument that the heat caused simultaneous failure of all vertical support columns. This leads me to a startling conclusion—if the 3M dampers had not been retrofitted, the WTC Twin Towers would have remained standing—at least longer, and possibly not collapsing at all. Moreover, I contend that the decision to retrofit the WTC with 3M dampers led to or certainly hastened the collapses on 9/11.

As the vertical columns buckled inward, the tremendous gravity load of the supported upper floors caused a collapse. Once started, the collapse became progressive. Each lower floor failed and fell upon being struck from above.

I submit that if the initial failure did not take place, the WTC Twin Towers would be standing today. Damaged, yes, but standing. Moreover, I submit that if proper heat-protective insulation had been in place, the ceiling trusses would not have failed. The insulation would have bought time. Time was required for the firefighters to respond and for the flames to dissipate as the fuel was consumed.

I will now address a way to resolve the insulation vs. no insulation question. Post-collapse photographs of World Trade Center debris abound and should reveal if various trusses and support columns had adhesively attached insulation, or if the trusses and support columns were devoid of insulation. I contend the latter. I also consider claims that all the insulation was dislodged to be preposterous. If the insulation was present throughout the structures, then virtually all structural remains will show insulation attached at least to some visible extent. Conversely, if numerous pieces of structural members have no insulation visible, I will have strengthened the no insulation hypothesis.

The above photograph by Andrea Booher/FEMA News shows World Trade Center beam debris. Permission to reproduce is greatly appreciated and acknowledged.

I look at the Andrea Booher photograph of pieces of World Trade Center structural debris, and I see zero evidence of heat-protective foam on the structural components. There is no evidence of insulation foam residue on the visible beams. The photographed structural debris was as clean as a hound's tooth.

The pseudo-experts explain this by saying that the foam insulation was there, but it turned to dust or blew away in the collapse. But if foam pieces were knocked off during the collapse, such as by abrasion or wind, some remnants and residues would still be present and visible. The beam portions protected by protrusions and joints would be expected to shelter foam residues as those sheltered areas had the benefit of some protection. Yet the many available photographs consistently show no foam or foam residues, whereas evidence of naked beams is universal. If spray-on foam was indeed applied, it would have been bonded to virtually all structural steel beams. Fireproofing involves the application of protective foam to all structural beams, not to just some fraction or select portions. Skeptics and foam-in-place advocates are invited to peruse the many available photographs.

In my life's journey, I have learned many lessons. One such lesson remains foundational to my philosophy: Look at firsthand evidence whenever possible as opposed to reading summary reports written by others. Courts of law routinely reject hearsay accounts and always seek firsthand accounts whenever possible. The architectural specifications do not constitute firsthand evidence because they are not the final say. What is specified by a designer or architect can be changed as construction progresses. It is folly to believe that a structure was built according to its original design on paper. It is common, even typical, for those in charge of construction to make changes and substitutions. What actually existed has the final say.

Experts and commissions, including American Society of Civil Engineers (ASCE) sanctioned bodies, performed post-mortem autopsies and studies on the World Trade Center. Numerous reports came to two common conclusions: The World Trade Center was built to and conformed with all applicable standards, and the World Trade Center structure remained intact and sound for so long even in the face of such blithering and unprecedented attacks.

I assert that the testimony of the WTC being built to all accepted standards was misleading, false, and self-serving. Next, the respective time spans that the World Trade Center towers remained standing were used to form conclusions. I prefer to categorize such conclusions as opinions, not conclusions. Those opinions were not based on any application of science or controlled experiment. Firsthand knowledge trumps opinions. The photographic evidence of post-collapse World Trade Center debris supports a no-foam conclusion. I consider such photographs as firsthand and beyond dispute. To that I also stand as an eyewitness. I testify that no spray-on foam was present during my 1975 inspection tour. I also bear witness that the structural engineer, Fred Chang, PE, asserted that all floors above the 20th were without heat-insulating foam.

The Towers Should Have Stood

When I have shared my World Trade Center story and testimony, I commonly get asked: If the heat-protective insulation had been in place, would the collapse have been prevented? To clarify the matter of the type of insulation, I will frame my answer assuming insulation with properties similar to asbestos-based insulation. From the long history of asbestos-based insulation, its insulating properties are well known.

Given this assumption, the undeniable response is to say that insulating foam would absolutely have bought time, substantial time for firefighting crews to respond. Moreover, additional time would have permitted the intense heat generated to diminish.

I will now render my opinion as to whether the tower collapses would have been prevented: My opinion is an emphatic *yes*. If the heat had been allowed to wane, the structural members would have held firm and the towers would have remained standing.

My reasoning is straightforward. The collapse occurred because a chain of events took place. The first structural members to fail were the overhead ceiling trusses within the fire zones. When the heated ceiling trusses failed, the supported concrete floors sagged. As the affected concrete floors sagged, tremendous mechanical advantage caused the exterior vertical columns to buckle inward.

Two separate mechanisms contributed loads to the vertical support columns, which were not designed to bear these added loads—whether heated or not. The two loads were:

- Inward pull forces exerted by the sagging floor
- A moment or lever-arm. The original specifications stipulated stationary pinned joints between the ends of the ceiling trusses and the vertical columns. However, a post-construction retrofit involved the installation of 10,000 viscous-elastic dampers in each tower. The dampers, supplied by the 3M Company of St.

Paul, Minnesota, altered the character of the connections between the trusses and the vertical support columns. The pinned joints were now no longer simple immobile pins, but rather joints that would support a moment. As each respective floor sagged, the combination of the pin and the 3M damper applied significant bending moments to the vertical support columns.

Once the perimeter vertical columns were locally bent or bowed inward, they were unable to support the load from above, thus causing a collapse to start. The failure of the vertical columns caused the drop of the overhead block of floors.

Following the attacks but before the respective collapses, numerous cameras recorded the sequence of events. Little doubt exists as to what happened next. Recordings of the collapse clearly show that both towers' upper blocks fell vertically. The WTC towers did not topple, but instead fell as if being hit on top by a sledgehammer. The collapses in both cases were progressive.

I am convinced to this day that the firefighting crews as well as police entered the WTC without the slightest forewarning that the WTC steel supporting beams and ceiling trusses were unprotected.

On December 23, 1975, my firsthand inspection tour unequivocally convinced me of one thing—the WTC Twin Towers were an immense death trap and public safety hazard. The seeds leading to the collapse on 9/11 were in place. Structural engineers, the owners of the buildings, and governmental oversight bodies all placed profits and pride ahead of public safety. I had no means to dictate public policy as per safety, but I opted to act for my own safety. I voted with my feet. I concluded, and rightly so, that civil and structural engineers were not qualified to design and construct tall buildings.

When dealing with fire trap situations, I would prefer to exit twenty-five years early, rather than be caught twenty-five minutes late. I exited the World Trade Center early, twenty-five years early, as opposed to being trapped within twenty-five minutes.

On that cold Tuesday afternoon of December 23, 1975, I departed the WTC and made my way to the subway entrance. As I walked, I glanced back over my shoulder. The towers of the WTC were massive by any human standard. I was in awe. As a human, I felt small and insignificant. That short walk to the subway entrance was an emotional moment in my life. I was filled with both incredible joy and profound sadness. Much of the joy came because I had finally gotten some straight answers about sway in tall structures.

Yet, what about the 50,000 unsuspecting people who entered that structural complex daily? There are times and situations in life when one feels helpless and powerless. That's what gave me my sadness. My professionalism as a mechanical engineer rendered me as mute as a stone. I had chosen to be a mechanical engineer—and to be conditioned to be polite and silent.

People in certain other professions are trained to be confrontational and adversarial. They are taught to be steadfast in the pursuit of one underlying thing—the truth. In stark contrast, mechanical engineers are conditioned to be cooperative and polite. Mechanical engineers are often clumped into teams of engineers while in the workplace. Outcomes are predicated on compromise, a compromise determined by majority consensus. Mechanical engineers seldom make waves. In contrast, lawyers are trained to fight. Investigative reporters are trained to seek out wrongs, and especially those who violate the public trust.

In excusing the civil engineers who built such a death trap, it is commonly said in their defense that nobody back then ever envisioned the 9/11 scenario. A decision was made to shortcut standards. The motivation was rooted in a combination of economics, a lust for power, and hubris. Environmental hazard concerns related to asbestos certainly played a role, but fail as an excuse for placing the public at risk. Unfortunately, thousands were trapped and paid the price.

Concluding Thoughts

My story and testimony as per the World Trade Center and September 11, 2001, will likely attract naysayers, critics, and doubters. The longer story and details to follow were written to make them work harder. I want my naysayers, critics, and doubters to have to work up a sweat, to have to rise early in the morning and struggle to comprehend systems theoretic principles. The lengthier story is filled with incredible details. At times, I use terms rooted in advanced optimal control concepts. The details, in my view, serve as corroboration of my story.

Reading the comprehensive version might give the impression that I, Richard Klein, am bitter—bitter that my ideas were rejected by so many and for so long. If you arrive at that conclusion, you have erred. I am and remain incredibly happy. Yes, I was rejected by the civil engineering profession, but that rejection changed the direction of my life. I went on to do many fun and rewarding things. This story about my encounters with the WTC and its collapse is but a minor sideshow in my life's work. At the end of the long story, I will share glimpses of my achievements and outcomes.

My oldest brother, Dr. Donald A. Klein (1935-2016), an expert in microbiology, stressed the importance of being ahead of one's time. Throughout my professional life, I have tried to live by that standard. I sought out problems where the practitioners were focused on traditional approaches.

I view myself as a product of the post-Sputnik era. In 1957 I was a college freshman studying engineering. In 1968, I defended my doctoral dissertation. My field of expertise was feedback systems theory. In a sense, I had become a rocket scientist. I had an arsenal of mathematical tools at hand to allow me to enter what were previously traditional fields.

Shortly following my entry into academia in 1968, I was attracted to the problem of controlling wind-induced sway in tall structures. I proposed using the wind itself to solve the wind-induced sway problem. My early proposals regarding feedback stabilization in structures were so radical and far ahead that the practitioners back then had no clue.

Even today, my abstract concepts regarding structural control remain puzzling to many. My early works in 1971 "The Active Control of Wind Induced Motion in Tall Structures" [3], and 1972 "Investigation of a Method to Stabilize Wind Induced Oscillations in Large Structures" [1] indeed represented pioneering landmarks. I take pride when I now see entire symposia and scholarly journals devoted to what are called smart materials and intelligent structures.

As I sit here almost half a century later, following my first forays into feedback stabilization of structures, I feel a sense of comfort in knowing that my ideas are being considered and even implemented at times. I wish I felt that same sense of comfort with regards to the World Trade Center towers.

Part 2 – The Rest of the Story

September 11, 2001, 8:14 a.m.: United Airlines Flight 175, a Boeing 767, carrying fifty-six passengers and nine crew members, departs fourteen minutes late from Logan International Airport in Boston, bound for Los Angeles International Airport. Five hijackers are on board. [4]

Who Is Richard E. Klein, PhD?

September 11, 2001, 8:42 a.m.: Flight 175 is hijacked above northwest New Jersey, about sixty miles northwest of New York City, continuing southwest briefly before turning back to the northeast. [4]

Disaster Strikes

On Tuesday, September 11, 2001, I was enjoying a beautiful sunny morning. My wife, Marjorie, had departed to her job teaching school. Both of my children had already moved out; my daughter, Victoria, was married and had set up family life, and my son, Tim, was in his senior year at Taylor University in Indiana. I was sitting at my dining room table doing some paperwork.

Then a friend telephoned and said, "They took down the World Trade Center." When my friend said "they," he was obviously referring to the enemies of America. He urged that I turn on the television. Heeding my friend's advice, I followed events as they were reported and watched as 9/11 became the modern day of infamy for many Americans.

Because of my interests in tall structures as well as my prior involvement with the World Trade Center, a huge store of memories resurged. My story of the WTC is lengthy and technical. It also has both legal ramifications and strong emotional implications. History reflects a tremendous death toll on 9/11. As a writer, I must select my words carefully, with the utmost deliberation and caution.

~~~~

I recently had a conversation with my grandson Noah about my personal experience with the World Trade Center Twin Towers. Now a recent college graduate, but just a kindergartener at the time of the attacks, he wanted to understand why the 9/11 terrorist attacks were so deadly.

"But Grandpa," he said, "if you knew the twin towers were unsafe, why didn't you speak up?"

"It's not so simple," I replied. "There are many reasons I wasn't able to tell this story until now. A lot of it has to do with the civil engineering culture in this country."

"I always thought you were a professor of mechanical engineering."

"That's right, Noah. Although I'm not a civil engineer, I became interested in tall building design in a roundabout way. In order to understand what led to my involvement with the World Trade Center, first you need to know how I became interested in skyscrapers, otherwise called quite simply in the engineering world, tall buildings. Let me start my story with my academic background."

A Cook's Tour of Two Professions

In this section, I give brief background sketches of two professions—civil engineering and a relatively new profession, feedback control engineering. I call this latter group engineers, but other descriptive words would be perhaps more appropriate. Think, for example, of feedback control theorists, or practitioners, or possibly gurus. Feedback control people are hard to quantify and describe because they live in an abstract world, a world of symbology and information management.

Throughout history, civil engineers have addressed the various tasks of creating an infrastructure for society to enjoy and benefit from. As humans created waste, waste disposal became an issue. Roman civil engineers constructed vast aqueduct systems, some of which remain standing today. The waste issue was solved, at least in the more enlightened societal structures. Likewise, Roman civil engineers leveled mountains and paved roads. Other early civil engineers understood the value of rock. The invention of the arch represented a breakthrough as it allowed greater spans between supports while keeping the individual rocks compressed. In the mid-eighteenth century came the invention of Portland cement. Somebody eventually got the idea of rebar, which included reinforcing steel bars within the cement. Yet another development was the idea that the reinforcing could be pre-stressed. The combination of concrete's resistance to compression along with the pre-tensioning of steel within made for an ideal structural component.

Civil engineering is a conservative profession. Taking a leap of faith into new ways of approaching problems isn't compatible with their culture. As a conservative profession, it is only natural for civil engineers to stay with methods and materials that are known, proven, and solid as rock.

Feedback control systems principles represent a relative newcomer to the world of engineering. An example of a feedback control system is cruise control in an automobile. Though riders experience the effect of a feedback control system when using cruise control, the system itself isn't a concrete thing.

Before the Industrial Revolution, mechanical power was primarily obtained from windmills and water mills. An important feedback control system was the flyball governor, developed in the 1600s to regulate speed. Just as windmills benefited from speed control as winds changed in direction and velocity, the flyball governor was adapted for speed regulation.

In the 1780s, James Watt made improvements to the flyball governor, especially as applied to steam engines. When the Industrial Revolution went into high gear with the widespread adoption of the improved steam engines (which were made possible by feedback control principles), the use of beasts of burden and slavery declined. James Clerk Maxwell gave feedback control its first mathematical underpinning with his 1868 treatise "On Governors."

Things moved along gradually, but then World War II loomed. An influx of growth as related to feedback principles, also referred to as servomechanisms, came about because of WWII. Note that the word *servomechanism* is derived from the Latin-based word servo implying slave or servant. Hence, a machine or device was able to do the work formerly done by beasts of burden, servants, or slaves.

In the late 1930s, President Roosevelt (FDR) realized, and wisely so, that the United States would be drawn into the war. He sensed that WWII was going to be a long and drawn-out war, and one that would ultimately be won or lost because of technology.

With this vision, Roosevelt appointed the most capable man he could identify to head up the United States' technological war efforts: Dr. Vannevar Bush (1890-1974). Dr. Bush was a sailing acquaintance of Roosevelt's. Roosevelt and Bush, being wealthy, had yachts and frequented the sailing community of Newport, Rhode Island.

By profession, Bush was an electrical engineer. At the time, he was the Dean of Engineering at the Massachusetts Institute of Technology (MIT). It is little wonder that MIT became the focal point of our nation's technological war efforts. Bush headed the combined work of about 6,000 mathematicians, engineers, and scientists who gave our nation things like radar, Loran navigation, inertial navigation (improved gyroscopes), improved vacuum tubes, code breaking, and advances in servomechanisms.

Roosevelt was correct in his predictions that the war would be long as well as waged and won with technology. Feedback control systems were foundational in the war effort, and the body of mathematical techniques expanded greatly during WWII.

The servomechanisms developments in America during WWII had been based largely on what is called the *frequency domain*. That came about because of the research of mathematician Dr. Harold Nyquist and electrical engineers Hendrik W. Bode and Harold S. Black in the 1920s and 1930s at Bell Telephone Laboratories.

The experimental work at Bell Telephone was based on frequency response excitation. The Nyquist Criterion, a mathematical theorem, solidified experimental findings regarding amplifier stabilization. The techniques developed prior to the war for telephone transmission stabilization were adopted and transported to help solve war-related problems like servomechanism positioning of large naval gun turrets. Hydraulics were used to accurately aim large naval guns on ships at sea. Feedback principles were applied to the servosystem reactions of ships to reduce ship rock. The mathematical techniques developed at Bell Telephone Laboratories assured the performance and the stability of the closed-loop positioning mechanisms. Thus, the pattern governing the future became clear: massive objects can be controlled and stabilized by feedback loops of information.

Manufacturing and technology in the United States boomed with new concepts stemming from servomechanisms advances coming out of WWII developments. These post-war contributions to feedback theory centered on *time domain control systems* and resulted from the integration of information, application, and technology.

The West did not know of Soviet advances until well after WWII when Soviet works were translated and made available. The Soviet advances in feedback control systems came from mathematicians, whereas the American developments were heavily influenced by the electrical engineers at Bell Laboratories. The Soviet launch of Sputnik on October 4, 1957 added more impetus for America to get its high-tech house in order.

The matrix algebra approach coming out of American universities was popularized by the work of Dr. Rudolph E. Kalman (1930-2016). Kalman's ideas contributed to the rapid progress of systems theory, which today draws upon mathematics ranging from differential equations to algebraic geometry.

The high-speed digital computer became increasingly viable as circuitry, chips, transistors, and solid-state devices emerged along with advances in computer memory. The ability to perform high-speed repetitive calculations permitted the automation of time-domain control systems.

In the two decades following the close of the war, the field of feedback control systems, previously known as servomechanisms, solidified. The Soviet and American approaches merged to become a unified body of knowledge. The principles and practices of feedback control systems became an important part of engineering educational curricula.

Getting My Doctorate in Feedback Control Systems

By the mid-1960s, many facets related to feedback control systems had come together. The area was so new that MIT and Purdue University were the only two major schools in the United States producing young PhDs in any significant quantity. In 1965, I was accepted by and began attending Purdue University to study control systems. Purdue's focus in feedback control systems in mechanical engineering was led by Dr. Rufus Oldenburger, a mathematician. During the WWII era, he served as the Director of Research at Woodward Governor Company in Rockford, Illinois. Upon joining Purdue's faculty, Oldenburger brought an immense background that combined both mathematics and industrial practices.

One reason for my attraction to tall structures related to my doctoral dissertation. At that time, significant advances had been made in control of lumped systems, meaning those systems modelled as rigid lumps. The control of wiggly systems—systems that are spatially flexible like wet noodles—remained largely an unchartered territory. The proper terminology is *distributed systems*, implying spatially distributed systems. Basically, think of trying to control something that is wiggly and flexible.

My thesis advisor at Purdue, Dr. Raymond E. "Gene" Goodson, suggested that I research *observability* of wiggly systems. The concepts of *observability* and *controllability* had become central to lumped feedback control systems, based on the work of Kalman [5] and others. After all, you can't start to control something until and unless you are first able to have some idea as to its current state.

Moreover, you can't know where something is (1) unless you take measurements, (2) if the system is *observable* when measured, and (3) you can somehow infer or compute the state based on those measurements. Another constraint is that only point measurements are feasible in practice and only at a restricted number of positions.

I accepted the challenge to study observability of wiggly systems and embarked on a quest to crack the observability problem.

My doctoral challenge was a backwards problem, also known as an inverse problem. I had to determine if the measurements outcome would permit one to tell or infer what caused the outcome. Another complication was that the inverse problem was inherently ill-posed, meaning that any measurement errors would produce large changes in the answers.

As an example, consider a taut vibrating string. For observability, what measurements must be taken on the vibrating string to assure uniqueness of the solution, to know the position and velocity of the string along its entire length? Several questions arise:

- Is it sufficient to position a sensor at some fixed location along the string and to measure the string's deflection at that designated interior point? Again, the objective is to infer and know the *state* of the vibrating string along its entire length.
- Can one accomplish this with fixed point measurements, or does one have to scan across (move continuously across) the string's entire length?
- Do we need more than one measurement, or will one measurement location suffice?
- With either one measurement or multiple measurements, where should the measurements (sensors) be placed?
- Is one location better than another?
- Is there a minimum time for the measurement, or will an arbitrary measurement duration suffice?

My dissertation became a study in unconventional boundary value problems in mathematical physics (aka *partial differential equations*). Although I was seeking a degree in mechanical engineering, my doctoral topic was a study in applied mathematics.

Several years of work allowed me to answer the above questions. My doctoral dissertation was somewhat atypical compared to most engineering dissertations. I never conducted an experiment. I never resorted to any form of simulation or digital computer analysis. I first defined observability for spatially distributed systems. Then I stated and proved two theorems.

My doctoral committee accepted my thesis. I answered the above questions for two important applications: the wave equation for a vibrating string and the parabolic heat equation (representing temperature distributions within a solid material). While I solved the wave equation problem in a few days, the tackling of the heat equation turned out to be far more challenging, requiring several years. I solicited and received help from a mathematics professor at another school, Dr. John R. Cannon, Jr. Following my entry into academia, Dr. Cannon and I published several papers related to the ill-posed inverse heat equation problem.

I finished and defended my doctoral dissertation at Purdue University on September 13, 1968 [6]. Dr. Goodson and I published my dissertation findings in *IEEE Transactions on Automatic Control* [7].

With my thesis defended—and reviewed favorably by my peers—I was now ready to find a job.

Becoming a Professor

It was late summer of 1968. As I approached my dissertation defense, I started the job search process. Marjorie and I set our sights on academia. We liked many things associated with teaching. Three were things called June, July, and August.

I prepared and mailed roughly fifty letters, each with an enclosed résumé. At the time, there were roughly 100 universities in the United States that had accredited mechanical engineering programs. I selected those fifty schools based on a simple criterion: I disliked the idea of living in a big city. In my estimation, if a city had a flying traffic reporter to detail rush-hour traffic jams, that city was scratched off the list. Oddly, only after reviewing the list one last time, did I add Illinois back onto the 'send a letter' category. I assumed I would be lucky to get even one job offer.

To my utter surprise, numerous mechanical engineering schools across the country were frantically trying to hire faculty in feedback control systems. New accreditation rules required schools in mechanical engineering to offer recently-mandated feedback control systems courses. About thirty schools nationwide expressed an interest in hiring me, offering interviews for an academic appointment. I even received telephoned job offers from three schools so desperate that the respective department heads bypassed the customary step of conducting an interview, making offers after receiving my résumé in the mail. Of the fifty letters sent out, all but two schools replied. About thirty expressed interest. Again, few candidates were in the marketplace. Most schools were under urgency due to the recent accreditation mandate. My fortunes were all working in my favor.

I traveled to and interviewed at five schools. All five made nearly identical offers in terms of starting salary. My wife Marjorie also interviewed for jobs as an elementary school teacher. Her salary offers, unlike mine, varied drastically. For example, teacher salaries in the South were half that of other regions. After looking at our combined offers, we selected Illinois.

On Monday, September 16, 1968, three days after my thesis defense, I stepped into a classroom as an Assistant Professor at the University of Illinois. By being at Illinois, Marjorie and I were close to family. Urbana-Champaign was a modest drive from Iowa and Marjorie's family farm roots. The University of Illinois in Urbana-Champaign was the most prestigious of the 'send a letter' list. Schools such as M.I.T., Stanford University, and the University of California at Berkeley were off my list because of my aversion to flying traffic jam reporters. Although Illinois was somewhat flat and dull, I had my pilot's license so we could hop into my club airplane and fly to more fun and scenic spots.

Richard E. Klein, standing on the wing of the Piper Cherokee PA-28-140, preparing to enter the cockpit. The aircraft, along with another similar one, was shared among twenty members of a flying club.

Marjorie and I assumed that we would be in Urbana-Champaign for three to five years. Then, suddenly and with little warning, the post-Sputnik era funding bust began in 1969 and continued into the early 1970s, changing the educational landscape. Also, the simultaneous Vietnam War and racial protests had devastating impacts on higher education in America. By the early 1970s, higher education—especially in technical areas—was contracting. Budget cuts and hiring freezes went into effect. The solution was to hunker down and remain in place, hoping for better days to return. The post-Sputnik boom times in education ended in 1969. Following a decade of hype, the moon walk became anti-climactic. A Peanuts cartoon featuring Snoopy summed it up. Snoopy said (paraphrased) as he lay dejected next to his doghouse, "If we can land a man on the moon, why then do I have to sleep in a doghouse?"

As I look back on my life, I see similarities to the way a banyan tree grows. I will now pick up and explain this thread, the analogy to the banyan tree. I started out studying mechanical engineering. I had enjoyed working on cars in high school but had experienced my fill of bruised knuckles. Therefore, I decided to design cars as opposed to working on cars that other people had designed. That was my justification for selecting mechanical engineering. During my undergraduate studies in mechanical engineering at Penn State, I became disenchanted. I simply deplored the study of thermodynamics and such mundane things. I wanted to design things, not be forced to endure things like steam tables, enthalpy, and entropy. Yes, before the advent of the digital computer and hand-held electronics, mechanical engineers carried around books of compiled steam properties. Other items they carried included slide rules, trigonometry tables, and logarithm tables. As a discouraged senior in mechanical engineering, I became focused on going into law school. I wanted to finish up, get my degree, and get out. I took the Law School Admission Test (LSAT) and received a high score. I envisioned a career in patent law. I applied to and was accepted at the University of Michigan law school, planning to enter in the fall of 1964. However, in my senior year of undergraduate studies at Penn State, I took a course in feedback control systems as an elective. I took it only because I needed the credits and nothing else was available. I struggled and even came close to failing. My grade was a D, but I had found my love and calling. I went on and got my MS and PhD degrees focusing on feedback control systems. My plans to attend law school were set aside.

Like the banyan tree, I sent a vine down. The vine touched ground, sank roots, and grew into a new trunk—the trunk of mathematics. My canopy of being a banyan tree spread wide. I look down from up top. My choice in target selection was premeditated; I'd select some juicy target and send down another vine that took root and become an additional trunk. My foray into structural control came about because I dropped down from a position founded in my canopy of mathematics and feedback control systems. Having the original trunk based in mechanical engineering provided additional support.

Upon entry into a new area or discipline, I made a concerted effort to immerse myself in the dialect and culture. I read journal articles. I attended societal meetings. I engaged in conversations with the inhabitants. In the case of my entry into structural control, I ended up spending several decades immersing myself in the civil engineering culture.

It seemed I had done everything possible to ready myself for dealing with civil engineers. But in the end, nothing could have prepared me for what I was met with.

Choosing Structural Control for My Research

As a young assistant professor at the University of Illinois in the late 1960s and early 1970s, despite the contraction in higher education funding, the world was my oyster. I was the beneficiary of the advances in feedback control systems made during WWII plus the post-war consolidation. Upon my entry into academia as a faculty member, I had theoretic mathematical tools in my bag that permitted me to address problems virtually at will. Moreover, as a theoretician, I required only paper, pencil, a quiet office, and time to think. I could do research and write papers without the need to run after grant money. The head of the department, Dr. Helmet L. Korst, recognized this as well. He instructed me to not pursue funding for research grants, and I did exactly as I was told, though this later had a negative impact.

As a college professor, I was expected to publish academic papers. After several years, I selected two primary topics for my research: structural control and ice age causation. In my early search for research topics, I deliberately looked for problem areas where confusion abounded and where the practitioners were still seeking answers using traditional (non-feedback) methods and thinking.

I was introduced to structural control because of a suggestion from a senior colleague, Dr. "Branny" *von* Turkovich (1924-2014) from the University of Illinois. Branny Turkovich was a colorful and interesting guy. He was Croatian by birth, but during WWII he lived in Naples, Italy. As southern portions of Italy fell into British control, Branny ended up being drafted into the British Royal Air Force. Upon the war's end and his discharge from the air force, he was a man without a country. He had served in the British Royal Air Force but wasn't a citizen of Britain or any other country. His former country of Croatia had disappeared in the turmoil following WWII. He lived in Spain as a student for a while before coming to America to work as a metallurgist in Milwaukee, Wisconsin. He then moved to Urbana, Illinois, where he earned doctorates in both physics and mechanical engineering. In his later career, he became Department Head of Mechanical Engineering at the University of Vermont. I deeply respected Branny Turkovich and owe a great deal to him.

In the spring of 1971, Dr. Turkovich, acting as my mentor, remarked to me that instead of focusing on abstract equations I should consider solving something real. Our offices were adjacent to each other, and our conversations often took place casually in the hallway. It was characteristic for Dr. Turkovich to make a brief comment on some topic as we might by happenstance meet.

Branny suggested I look at sway problems in modern tall skyscrapers in one off-the-cuff interchange. It wasn't more than a sentence or two. I'm certain that Turkovich had been motivated by reports then circulating of unwanted sway in some newly constructed structures, typified by the recently completed Sears Tower in Chicago, Illinois. Turkovich proposed that I turn to an application that was physical and that existed as a problem.

Construction advances in the 1960s and the subsequent decades led to steel-framed structures with non-load-bearing cladding. Examples included the Sears Tower in Chicago, the John Hancock Tower in Boston, the Citicorp Center in New York, and the World Trade Center Twin Towers in New York. There was a potential research topic hidden in these modern (for the time) buildings, I just had to figure out what it was.

Theorizing the Use of an Intelligent Finger

The words *mechanism* and *structure* refer to two types of mechanical things: those that have internal moving parts and those that just stand still or remain fixed. Two contrasting illustrations are the ticking wall clock and an ancient Egyptian pyramid. The clock can be classified as a mechanism, while the pyramid can be classified as a structure.

To say that we will control the motion in a structure at first suggests an oxymoron. Why would you need to control the motion of something that doesn't move? This would be a good point, except that steel has replaced rock as a primary construction material in modern tall buildings. These modern steel-framed structures depend on steel beams that can undergo slight changes in shape. Furthermore, if a steel-framed structure is subjected to variable side loads, such as aerodynamic excitations (i.e., wind), the structure will respond, meaning that the structure will sway. A complication that arises is that steel-framed tall structures move and tend to bounce back. They also have minimal internal energy dissipation. The question is how to apply a stopping action to a tall structure that is devoid of something to push against. A solution to tame (or at least minimize) that behavior is essential.

The owners and architects of tall buildings go to great lengths to see that the public is unable to detect any movements within the structure. In a tall building, movements lead to accelerations that are small in magnitude, almost to the point of being imperceptible by the human occupant. The movements aren't harmful and usually pose no danger. While an occupant may not be aware of the motion of the structure, he may nonetheless suspect that something is amiss.

One practice addressing side-to-side movements is to eliminate telltale signs such as long suspended draperies or hanging chandeliers that might swing. A harder motion to conceal from occupants is the torsional twisting of a structure. The sideways twisting is often slow, but yet the horizon seems to be moving back and forth, especially if the human is seated and observing a fixed point on the distant horizon.

Wind-induced vibration in tall and slender modern structures represents a challenging and somewhat unexpected problem. Vibration suppression is difficult to achieve because the structure is sufficiently compliant, the structure inherently has scant internal damping, wind as an exciting force is hard to predict as it varies in force and direction, and there is nothing to push against. It is trivial to arrest motion if one can exert an external sideways and opposing force on the building, but tall, cantilevered buildings don't permit easy pushbacks. With the advent of modern steel-framed structures, the matter of stabilization became increasingly important.

At that point in my career, I had joined various societies, one being the Society for Industrial and Applied Mathematics (SIAM). A day or two following the challenge by Branny Turkovich, I received information about a forthcoming SIAM meeting in Denver. The announcement gave a listing of accepted papers that would be presented. Just by reading the title of one paper, a candidate solution to the puzzle came to me in a flash. As is often the case of synthesis, two mental images happened to closely coincide so that the two ideas were combined to form a new idea.

The paper that inspired me was "Controllability of Linear Oscillatory Systems Using Positive Controls," [8] by Dr. James A. Yorke and a student of his, both from the University of Maryland. In it, they proved that a dynamic system with oscillatory behavior, thus an oscillatory structure, would be *controllable* as defined by Kalman [5], using positive (one-directional) forces. The implication was that a swaying object can be made to come to rest even if one can only exert forces limited to one direction.

To add historical perspective, Yorke went on in his career to achieve fame as the founder of modern chaos theory. See the book by Gleick [9].

Yorke's impetus suggesting positive control forces led me to believe that a structure can be brought to rest by a controlled and manipulated smart force. The smart force would be like a fictitious yet intelligent hand that could apply a controlled force onto the swaying structure.

A child on a backyard swing is an example. The adult characteristically exerts timed (smart) pushes in one direction. When the applied one-directional pushes coincide with the child's forward velocity, the amplitude of swing increases and the child swings higher and faster. Conversely, when the parent or adult reverses the timing of the pushes, by pushing against the velocity (when the child is coming backwards towards the adult), the child soon comes to rest.

In an analogous manner, if an intelligent pushing finger can be applied to the structure by exerting an opposing force to the sway's velocity (assuming sway in the along-wind direction), the unwanted sway can be dissipated. This strategy works even if the exerted force is one-directional, just as in the case of the child on a backyard swing.

Moreover, to accomplish this goal, I assert that the wind itself is available and capable of becoming that intelligent finger. The next question becomes one of finding or creating a suitable finger to do the pushing. In the sketch below, I show a generic leading-edge appendage in the finger "on" or pushing position. That appendage need not be huge. Even small changes in geometry when applied to sharp leading edges can achieve substantial changes in drag coefficients. This applies for bluff bodies (i.e., structures with a large perpendicular front face) in subsonic flow conditions (i.e., when the wind speed is less than the speed of sound), which is the case with tall buildings.

One fact is abundantly clear. Even for small amplitudes of sway in a building, the full effort of the "finger" remains. Because the modulated component (appendage) of the building's aerodynamic drag force remains in full, the amplitude of motion diminishes rapidly. In stark contrast, viscous dampers, to be discussed later, diminish in effectiveness as the sway amplitude diminishes.

Tall, cantilevered structures, especially modern structures erected with steel framing, are indeed dynamic and are much like musical instruments. When struck or excited, they tend to resonate at specific and predictable frequencies. The point is that energy, when induced into the structure, will become associated with the structure's natural frequencies. Piano strings and violin strings resonate at specific frequencies when they are struck. Drum heads and cymbals, in contrast, exhibit a broad mix of frequencies when struck. Tall, cantilevered structures are tuned instruments, not noise-makers. In one sense this is bad because when the amplitudes of the tuned frequencies are highly excited, they can become large.

The good news is that the control strategy options are far easier to implement, especially if feedback principles are employed. Assume that a smart feedback controller is in place on a building. The control of the building and its unwanted energy becomes a simple task as long as one can dissipate energy from the excited frequencies. Moreover, although structures have many natural frequencies, the reality is that in most cases only the lower or fundamental frequencies are excited. The high frequencies don't often get excited, and if they do, they often have adequate internal damping. In short, it suffices to focus stabilizing control at a limited number of frequencies, and these are often the lower structural frequencies. The application of feedback control stabilization is easy. This attribute of feedback control systems is known and obvious to the residents dwelling in the black hole, whereas those outside the black hole of feedback systems operate in darkness.

Understanding Structural Control

September 11, 2001, 8:52 a.m.: On board Flight 175, a flight attendant calls a United Airlines office in Chicago, reporting that the flight had been hijacked, both pilots had been killed, a flight attendant had been stabbed, and the hijackers were probably flying the plane. [4]

The Tragedy of 9/11

At first, it seemed like debris. Large objects were falling from the top of the World Trade Center's north tower, just a few minutes after American Airlines Flight 11 hit.

The story of the victims who jumped to their deaths is the most sensitive aspect of the 9/11 tragedy. Photographs of people falling to their deaths shocked the nation. Most newspapers and magazines ran only one or two photos, then published no more. *USA TODAY* [10] ran one photo on November 16, 2001. Still, the images resonate. Many who survived or witnessed the attack say the sight of victims jumping is their most haunting memory of that day.

It was worse than people realize.

USA TODAY estimated that at least 200 people jumped to their deaths that morning, far more than can be seen in the photographs taken that morning.

For those who jumped, the fall lasted ten seconds. They struck the ground at just under 150 miles per hour—not fast enough to cause unconsciousness while falling, but fast enough to ensure instant death on impact. People jumped alone, in pairs and in groups.

Intense smoke and heat, rather than flames, pushed people into this horrific choice. Flight 11 struck the 94th through 98th floors of the north tower, shooting heat and smoke up elevator shafts and stairways in the center of the building. Within minutes, it would have been very difficult to breathe. That drove people to the windows 1,100 to 1,300 feet above ground.

Some who fell didn't jump. Witnesses say a few people seemed to have stumbled out of broken windows obscured by smoke. But most say those jumping appeared to make a conscious choice to die by falling rather than from smoke, heat, or fire. Ultimately, they were choosing not whether to die but how to die. Nobody survived on the floors from which people jumped.

~~~~

"Noah, are you following my explanations?" I asked. I sensed that my grandson was a bit confused with all the technical jargon.

"Maybe not all of it," he admitted. "Can we jump ahead to the easy part?"

"We could, but then you wouldn't truly understand how we got there," I said. "It's important to go through it step-by-step because all the pieces fit together. Here, let me try to explain the concepts of structural control with some analogies. That always seemed to help my undergraduate students."

Noah settled back in his chair, his eyes focused on me. I still had his attention. If he could just stay with me a bit longer, he'd understand everything: the problem, the poor solution, and the inevitable fallout. Not to mention the greed, arrogance, and corruption. He really was in for an intriguing revelation.

Dogs and Cats

Other than each having a tail and four feet, cats and dogs have few common behavioral traits. When at rest, cats tend to remain rigid and fixed, except possibly for a twitch in the tail. In contrast, when a dog stands wagging its tail, the whole dog wags. Recall the old expression "the tail wags the dog." Tall, steel-framed structures behave akin to dogs. If any part wiggles, that wiggle is shared throughout the structure. Yes, tall structures are anchored in place, connected to a solid foundation. But when wind or seismic excitation occurs, the entire structure participates.

This characteristic trait of cantilevered steel-framed structures allows for a simple approach to control sway. Just as the tip of the dog's tail exhibits amplified motion, so is the movement of the top of the structure amplified. In mathematical physics, this is referred to as the *free boundary condition*. Because the goal in structural control is to dissipate energy, it suffices to apply a retarding action to the tip of the "tail": the free boundary condition. The top of a tall structure represents a free boundary condition. The vibrational mode shapes within the structure are always at a local maximum at the free boundary condition.

A foundational principle in feedback systems theory and practice is to use the simplest of available models so long as the outcome makes sense. The entire premise of feedback control systems is to not solve problems *per se*, but rather to bound and thus limit the possible outcomes. For example, assume that feedback can be incorporated to dissipate energy from a structure. The energy in the structure will diminish without a detailed knowledge of the internal specifics of the structure.

For implementation of a feedback control, one can accomplish this by doing two things: place the motion sensor(s) at the free boundary condition (at the top of the structure) and collocate the smart actuator or controlling finger with the motion sensor(s).

In rough terms, half a century ago we lacked access to many electronics that today we take for granted. The average smart phone of today has more computing power than what was housed in extensive mainframe computer centers when we sent a man to the moon. With the advent of GPS devices to know a building's sway with precision and supporting electronics, the ability to implement smart feedback systems on structures is virtually off-the-shelf. Implementation of concepts proposed nearly fifty years ago is within reach. The technology is at hand and available.

It suffices to place both sensor and actuator at the free boundary condition. The structural modelling assumptions are irrelevant for the outcome. These conclusions assume a relatively weak control action. If the control action, in contrast, would be gargantuan, that magnitude of force would alter the structure's shape. This is a fine point and not likely to exist in practice, but it needs to be stated.

Flies and Elephants

In a discussion with Dr. Nick Isyumov in 1987, he asserted that a fly on an elephant can't materially alter the aerodynamic drag forces on the elephant. At that time, Dr. Isyumov was the director of the world-leading boundary layer wind tunnel at the University of Western Ontario. In the summer of 1987, I was invited to visit the facility. I met with both Dr. Isyumov and Dr. Alan G. Davenport, the founder and original director. Dr. Isyumov was certainly a person of stature in the profession, so his remarks had to be taken with considerable seriousness. Essentially, Dr. Isyumov was making a point about order of magnitude. An elephant is big; a fly is tiny. So how could any outcome depend on what the fly did?

Mathematicians such as Dr. James A. Yorke, who became the founder of modern chaos theory, shook up traditional mathematical thinking as demonstrated with the advent and emergence of chaos theory. The entire fly and elephant question hinges on *sensitive dependence*, otherwise know as the butterfly effect. In chaos theory, the butterfly effect states that a small change in one state can result in large differences in a later state, deriving its name from the metaphorical example of a tornado or hurricane being influenced by the flapping of the wings of a distant butterfly several weeks earlier. In my dissertation findings, I encountered sensitive dependence. In the ensuing years, I met Dr. Yorke at a society meeting and expressed my thanks to him for his papers with Bob Bramer and Steve Saperstone, two of his students. Both papers dealt with controllability of oscillatory systems with positive (unidirectional) forces. During my discussion with Yorke, I informed him of my application of his concepts to structures. Yorke, who falls into the category of rather eccentric mathematicians, was somewhat taken aback. The zenith for a mathematician of Yorke's stature is to prove something so abstract that it has no chance of applicability to anything real. In my estimation, based on his body language, Yorke appeared taken aback that something he had done had resulted in a possible practical application.

My reply to Dr. Isyumov related to the fly and the elephant was lengthy. Everything hinges on two basic factors: the shape of the elephant and the position of the fly on the elephant. I stated that my proposition to incorporate active intelligent appendages on a structure was viable given several conditions, albeit conditions that most common elephants fail to meet. After all, elephants and skyscrapers don't have too much in common. For example, we seldom see elephants vibrating because of wind induced excitations. The conditions I envisioned on my metaphorical elephant and flies included:

- a tall, bluff body with sharp corners
- the tendency to be reactive to fluctuations in the surrounding aerodynamic pressures
- low internal damping, thus being similar in damping to a modern steel-framed tall structure
- a sufficient number of appendages that can be located along the leading sharp edges
- appendages that are organized, intelligent, and will obey commands from a centralized controller or logic system
- sufficient internal and external sensors capable of acquiring signal information regarding positions, velocities, accelerations, strains, prevailing wind directions, and possibly air pressures on surfaces (all of which sense information that is available in real-time)

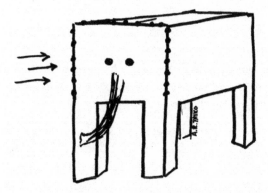

In the sketch above, the legs are a bit short. My rectangular elephant would be much taller, just as skyscrapers are tall.

The resolution of the fly and elephant question remains open, but I am confident that an answer will someday come. However, I predict that the present generation of civil engineers will not be the ones to answer other than in the negative.

Cows and Donkeys

As the years went by, I received invitations to speak and to serve on various committees and panels. At a civil engineering discussion panel in Indianapolis in 1991, I outlined several mitigation approaches [11] for the stabilization of large structures. The meeting was sponsored by the American Society of Civil Engineers (ASCE).

As a seated panelist, I was given the opportunity to make remarks to the assembled audience. I devoted my presentation time to an overview of my past twenty years (1971-1991) of research in structural control, with an emphasis on the potential that existed for advances based on application of systems theoretic principles.

I referred to one approach as the "cow-donkey theory of structural control."

My prepared visuals included a cartoon with a donkey tethered to a cow. As a clarification, when this is professionally done, the tether on the cow is usually attached either to a secure backpack or a halter on the donkey. Unlike my cartoon sketch above, neither animal is tied around its neck.

The audience, composed mostly of civil engineers, openly laughed. Even Dr. Nick Isyumov, the panel's moderator, quipped at the end of my presentation, saying that I had missed my true calling in life: to be a stand-up comedian.

The analogy of the cow and donkey stemmed from my knowledge of taming cattle. That knowledge had its source in the farm roots of my father-in-law, George A. Maxwell, who farmed near Davenport, Iowa. Because he specialized in dairy cattle and also owned some beef cattle, he was familiar with what he considered an effective, simple, and easy way to "break" a calf to be halter trained. I use the word calf, but in beef circles the animal can be perhaps as heavy as 1,000 pounds. One must not harm or unnecessarily stress the animal, and certainly the handler of the cattle must also be safe, since both dairy and beef cattle must be submissive in the show ring.

Photo used with permission

An errant cow or steer can be made docile if it is tethered to a donkey and then both are turned out to pasture. Thirst becomes an incentive for the cow to follow the donkey to water. The cow will drink only when the donkey drinks, and so it goes. The differences in temperament between the two animals will soon train the errant cow or steer to be led in the show ring. In most cases this happens after only a day in the pasture.

As many as ninety percent of beef cattle in the show ring have been broken to lead using the cow-donkey procedure, and a business even exists where farmers will rent out donkeys for that specific purpose.

In regard to controlling structural sway, adjacent structures tethered together can produce dramatic results in terms of energy dissipation as long as the respective structural temperaments are different. Unlike the cow-donkey, the interconnection of structures should include a dissipative connecting link, hence some form of damper. In mathematical terminology, the requirement on the structures for this to work was that the natural frequencies of the respective structures be distinct (dissimilar).

The four towers of the Harumi Island Triton Square complex in Tokyo, Japan are interconnected with dissipative links that also serve as walkways. Photo courtesy of the Global Tall Building Database of the Council of Tall Buildings and Urban Housing.

In 2001, the Harumi Island Triton Square complex in Tokyo was designed and built based on my concepts. These very same concepts evoked open laughter from the ASCE Structures audience in Indianapolis in 1991. The assembled audience of about fifty civil engineers was laughing mostly at me, not with me. The concepts and mathematical underpinnings of my research thrusts were and remain foreign to the bulk of American civil engineers. When I taught at the University of Illinois, mechanical and electrical engineering students were required to take ordinary differential equations following calculus. In contrast, civil engineering students had weaker alternative options, notably a watered down course in linear algebra. The highlight of that course was being able to invert a 3x3 matrix. In my three decades of teaching system control classes, I had hundreds of electrical, nuclear, aeronautical, and agricultural engineering students, but not one civil engineering student. Civil engineers as a profession tend to lack the requisite mathematical background to master system theoretic principles.

The towers of the Triton Square complex are interconnected by energy-absorbing walkways. Each of the towers was designed to sway at its own distinct frequency. Although not obvious in the photograph, the difference in the respective sway periods resulted because each of the interconnected towers was of a distinct and different height. Each tower acts as a stabilizing anchor, or donkey, for the companion towers, or calves.

From my perspective, Asian civil engineers are considerably more advanced than their American counterparts. For example, tall buildings in Japan and Singapore are necessarily designed with strict earthquake mitigation because they sit on the Pacific Rim. Entire symposia, most recently in China and Southeast Asia, are devoted to the topic of structural control, smart materials, and intelligent buildings.

In the case where asymmetrical buildings aren't feasible (such as when they are already built) or in the case of a single building, you'll need another solution.

Understanding Aerodynamic Drag and Wind-Induced Sway

September 11, 2001, 8:59 a.m.: Flight 175 passenger Brian Sweeney leaves a message via airphone to his wife Julie: "Jules, this is Brian, listen, I'm on an airplane that's been hijacked. If things don't go well, and it's not looking good, I just want you to know I absolutely love you, I want you to do good, go have good times, same to my parents and everybody, and I just totally love you, and I'll see you when you get there. Bye, babe." [4]

Evacuation of the South Tower

On that fateful day, many occupants of the South Tower of the World Trade Center had seen what had happened in the North Tower and thus chose to evacuate as a precaution. However, for the seventeen minutes between the impacts of Flight 11 and Flight 175, it had not yet been determined that a terrorist attack was unfolding, and as a result the tower's owner and management, the Port Authority, spread the word via the building's intercom system and security guards that workers in the South Tower should remain in their offices.

A package deliverer told reporters he heard the first crash and that as he evacuated he heard, "The building is secure. The safest place is inside; stay calm and do not leave." Others who ignored the message were met with officials in the lobby who told them to return to their respective floors.

In a recorded radio conversation about two minutes after the first plane hit, the director of the South Tower stated, "I'm not going to do anything until we get orders from the Fire Department or somebody." This was done in order to avoid overcrowding on the plaza and concourse levels, which was feared would slow the evacuation and rescue operations in the North Tower. Regardless, thousands of people continued to evacuate the South Tower. In the uppermost section of the South Tower between the 78th Floor Sky Lobby and the Observation Deck on the 107th and 110th floors, there were an estimated 2,000 employees.

~~~~

"Okay, now I think I understand the potential for control systems and how they can be used in theory to tame tall structures," Noah said. "The whole point is to stop the buildings from swaying by getting rid of the energy that comes from the wind. Tethering buildings together like a cow and a donkey can help dissipate energy. A small appendage added to the top of a tall building can have a big impact in damping wind sway, just like a tiny fly can have an impact on a huge elephant."

"Of course, buildings aren't animals and those analogies are pretty rough, but I hope they gave you some insight." I'm proud of the bright young man my grandson has become.

"I don't understand how tall buildings can be wobbly, though," Noah said. "They seem pretty stable to me."

"Some are steady and some are wobbly," I said. "It all depends on the design of the building and how it handles the forces of wind blowing across and around it. Dealing with wind is also tricky. Winds change or are variable in direction. Wind gusts are hard to predict. A nice attribute of feedback systems is that the feedback system can alter or change its feedback strategy to adjust as the wind conditions shift and change. My MS thesis at Pennsylvania State University dealt with a concept called adaptive control. As conditions external to a plant change, the control system can change to adapt itself. Thus, a controlled device can adapt itself to function better as the external conditions change. The amount and type of building sway also depends on the vortex shedding of structures around it." I noticed Noah's eyebrows furrow at the mention of the term "vortex shedding."

"So... did wind sway contribute to the collapse of the towers on September 11?"

"Yes and no," I answered. "Wind itself will not knock over a tall building. But it causes the building to sway, which is unpleasant for the building's occupants. Therefore, engineers must address this problem, preferably before construction."

"And, based on your tone and the fact you're writing this book," Noah said, "I'm guessing the engineers did not do that."

"You are correct. The need to fix the sway problem in the towers after construction had already started resulted in a chain reaction of poor decisions that ultimately led to the collapse of the towers." I paused, letting this sink in. "To better explain, I'll discuss the concept of aerodynamic drag and the related concept of vortex shedding. But first, let's talk about shaping appendages."

What Are Shaping Appendages?

Aerodynamic drag forces on a bluff body, i.e., an object with a perpendicular front, can vary with the geometry or shape of the body. If one can alter the geometry of a structure, independent of its projected frontal area, one can then alter the forces created by its aerodynamic drag.

In recent years, attention has been given to aerodynamic drag reduction on highway vehicles as a means of reducing fuel consumption.

Over-the-road truck-trailers now achieve significant drag reduction with shaping and rounding appendages.

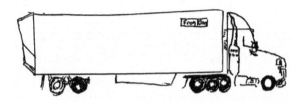

In the sketch above, the truck-trailer has three modifications designed to reduce the aerodynamic drag:

- A rounding baffle is mounted over the truck's cab
- Flaps at the end of the trailer extend backward but inward at a slight angle
- Skirts fill in the sides under the length of the trailer

None of these shaping features increase the truck's projected frontal area. These lightweight, relatively inexpensive features dramatically reduce the overall air drag and favorably impact highway fuel economy. Reports of fuel consumption savings of thirty percent are commonplace. If these shaping appendages had no effect, truck designers wouldn't use them.

~~~~

"Grandpa, I agree that large trucks can be modified to decrease aerodynamic drag, thereby saving fuel," said Noah. "What confuses me is that your appendages retrofitted or added onto structures will increase drag—not decrease it. It doesn't make much sense."

"Noah, I can achieve my goal either way. I can decrease drag; or I can increase drag. The important thing is that with feedback, I can turn the drag changes on and off at my choosing. Everything boils down to dissipating energy. Just as in the case of a child on a swing. I can reduce the sway by applying a push when the child or building is coming back or against the finger's or the wind's direction. If I increase the drag, as I have proposed, fuel economy is a moot point. A tall building isn't being driven down a highway. Instead, it is anchored in place on hopefully a solid foundation. A little more steady drag might cause the building at the top to shift three inches or even three feet. The shift is a steady change. The occupants don't know and frankly aren't even aware in the slightest."

I went on, "Envision a swing or a building. The wind and drag forces have two components, just like electricity: a steady component and an alternating component. I will refer to these as DC and AC. Aerodynamic drag isn't electrical, but we can see the analogy easily. The DC component of wind only causes a steady and small shift of the child or building. Because I propose to control and manipulate the AC or variable component of drag, I can time its on-off or switching to maximize the energy drain. So long as I am extracting energy, meaning the sway energy, the child and/or building will swing or sway less. The ability to dissipate energy in an oscillating structure is incredibly effective. It takes just small changes in the modulated or manipulated AC component to achieve significant sway energy reduction."

"But Grandpa," said Noah, "what you said sounds so contradictory. You said that even small changes in a structure's aerodynamic drag can dissipate lots of energy. I don't see the logic in that."

I realized that I needed to go back a little deeper, to build some foundational concepts. I needed to review the concept of work as defined and used in physics.

"In its most simple terms, work is defined as the product of force times distance. Whenever force is applied and something moves, work is being done. In a situation of wind creating drag forces on a building, whenever the building moves, such as in the same direction as the wind, then the wind is performing work. Energy is being put into the building. Conversely, when the building sways or moves into the wind, the building is giving up its energy. In the case of a swaying building, energy is being added and subtracted. The energy being added is equal to what gets subtracted provided the aerodynamic forces or drag forces remain constant. With each cycle of sway, as the building goes back and forth, energy is being added and then given up. But think of a tax collector. If the tax collector's hand is outstretched, and charging for each and every sway or bridge crossing, it doesn't take too long before the tax collector has accumulated a heap of money. The appendage control scheme acts like a tax collector. Recall that the building is swaying whenever it is windy. The control strategy's hand is out there—extracting a percentage. Pretty soon the building ends up with empty pockets—the building has lost its energy. Whenever you lose money at a rate faster than it can come in, pretty soon you are broke. In a similar manner, pretty soon the building has given up all or most of its energy.

"An amazing thing happens when we can vary the drag forces at our command. Moreover, we need to concentrate on the AC component, the portion of the wind load that we can change. The bigger DC or steady component is immaterial because it doesn't produce any net work per sway cycle.

"By timing the changes in drag force to be out-of-phase with the direction of velocity, we can maximize energy dissipation from the structure. Also, we can get the most bang out of the buck if we grab and use everything available. The most effective way to dissipate energy from within a structure is to maximize the rate of energy extraction. The best way to do this is to time the appendage changes for when the structure switches its direction of movement, and to use everything we have. That is why my designs are based on a simple on-off switching command. What I'm going to say next might seem absurd. Timing is crucial. The changes in drag must be out of phase with the building's swaying. If we had a reversed sign, thus the wrong timing, the appendage drag changes would amplify the building's sway—not decrease the sway. Of course, our electronic command logic won't permit that to happen.

"In my 1972 ASME paper [1], my simulations showed that sway energy could be cut by ninety percent if the drag could be varied by as little as five percent. Recall that over-the-road trucks with shaping appendages achieve thirty percent drag reduction with shaping appendages. I consider getting five percent changes to be a breeze.

"Gee, Grandpa," said Noah. "I see that the AC component holds the answer. I also see that an on-off or bang-bang control approach would be simple to implement. In my robotic studies, it would be called a binary command decision."

~~~~

Another benefit of active aerodynamic appendages is that they can confuse and thereby disorganize vortex shedding, when present. Recall that golf balls have little dimples for one reason—the dimples act to break up and confuse vortex shedding and thus the trailing wake. Golf balls go farther because they are designed with dimples.

Yet another advantage of aerodynamic appendage control concerns how loads, when acting as the intelligent finger, spread or distribute the finger's push on the building. Point or concentrated loads are avoided. The distributed action of the finger means that less reinforcing is required.

In the case of bluff objects, the object can be designed to have increased drag. It is easier to increase drag as opposed to decreasing drag, especially on civil engineering structures.

Clearly, the converse to streamlining of bodies holds also true. Objects can be reverse-designed to increase aerodynamic drag. Modern airliners routinely use drag increasing devices called spoilers when landing.

Leading and trailing edges can be made sharper with smart appendages, meaning active appendages that can be manipulated per feedback principles. These sharper edges can be utilized to increase aerodynamic drag, thus slowing the motion.

The Water Table Visualization

Theories are great, but proof is needed before theories can be applied to real-life problems. I was able to prove my manipulated appendages control theory by using a water table visualization experiment.

Fluid dynamics explain that drag is dictated by what is referred to as the *coefficient of drag*, which varies with geometry. The fluids laboratory at the University of Illinois in the 1970s had a water table, also called a free-surface water table. Without going into the technical detail, the overall idea is that two-dimensional water flow can provide visualization or close approximate representation of two-dimensional subsonic flow conditions. I used the water table at the University of Illinois to conduct scale model flow visualization experiments.

The above water table visualization shows a two-dimensional flow of air moving past a rectangular building. There is no appendage. The simulated air flow is from the right going to the left. Note the height of the turbulent region above the building.

The two photographs below show the change in the dimension and character of the turbulence depending on the orientation of the smart (hence manipulated) aerodynamic appendage. As you can see, placing the appendage at the structure's leading edge as well as extending it forward of the building's frontal face yields greater effectiveness.

The water table flow visualization results were strongly positive.

The darker areas of turbulence stood out visually as liquid laundry dye was poured judiciously into the flow stream. The water table was configured on a plate glass surface—over which the water flowed—with a large mirror underneath at a 45-degree angle to permit photography. The ceiling area above the water table was illuminated white to provide a proper background. The water table apparatus resembled a televised cooking studio with a mirror overhead to allow the audience to remain seated while being able to see what is happening on the table.

I regret that as educational and research views changed over the years, the water table apparatus at the University of Illinois was discarded. It was replaced with, of course, computer stations and similar high-tech virtual reality devices. But of course, they didn't ask me for my opinion.

Dr. Helmet L. Korst provided certain valuable insights during my experimentation process. His specialization was gas and fluid dynamics. His expertise in fluid flow matters was world-respected and beyond question. Korst made the following summary statement: "The coefficient of drag on a bluff body (assuming subsonic, incompressible flow) can be approximated by the width or characteristic dimension of the downstream turbulence."

As confirmed by my water table visualization experiments, small changes in leading edge geometry resulted in significant variations of the amount of downstream turbulence. After I conducted my water table experiments, I shared the findings with Dr. Korst, and he agreed with my conclusion that manipulated appendages, even if small compared to the structure's size, can cause significant changes in the structure's drag coefficient.

Understanding Vortex Shedding

One of the more common excitation modes in tall, slender structures is vibrational motion that arises because of *vortex shedding.* Vortex shedding essentially amounts to periodic eddies being formed from alternating sides of the structure.

In the sketch above, the fluid is flowing from right to left. The eddies formed display the characteristic pattern of alternating swirls.

It is common in flexible structures that the alternating pressure fluctuations on the structure will cause lateral oscillations (sideways movements) of the structure. The above depiction shows a cylindrical body. Vortex shedding can also occur with other bluff shapes.

When vortex shedding is present, the resulting structural motion is typically cross-wind, but can also be torsional oscillation. As an alternative to arresting motion caused by a continued excitation source, an approach would be to defeat or otherwise confuse the vortex shedding before it can grow and then inflict its damage. The idea is to nip the smaller vortices in the bud before they can grow into big vortices.

The nipping strategy could be relatively straightforward. Active spoiler tabs and/or bleeds can be placed and manipulated to confuse and disorganize the vortex shedding. Of course, stationary geometry changes can be considered as well, such as the use of dimples in golf balls, which reduces vortex shedding to about half that of a smooth ball.

I began looking at these options and approaches in the 1980s. Some years later, in the early 1990s, I became aware of the work of Williams and Amato [12] who experimented with control of vortex shedding by the incorporation of bleeds passing through the structure itself. The idea of disrupting the generation of vortex shedding would appear to have potential.

My Idea Takes Shape

Now I was ready to envision what my theoretical smart appendage might look like in practice. It was obvious to me that, if one can actively change a structure's shape using feedback, then aerodynamic drag forces can be modulated to suit. The manipulated component (i.e., the smart appendage), when timed to be out of phase with the sway velocity, will efficiently dissipate the structure's vibrational energy (the energy associated with movement). The switching action or command is timed to extract energy from the structure. Manipulated aerodynamic smart force becomes the arresting force. The steady component of drag is of no concern, as steady forces don't cause dynamic excitations. It was also obvious to me that the wind that is causing building sway can also, in turn, be exploited to arrest the unwanted sway.

Unlike over-the-road trucks, a control strategy can be employed in the case of tall structures by increasing the drag based on smart feedback commands. The goal is to be able to modulate, thus manipulate, upon a feedback command, the applied drag forces. For civil engineering structures this can be achieved by incorporating smart drag control. Once the drag can be varied, hence manipulated, by command, the sway in the along-wind direction can be reduced quite dramatically. I can achieve my objective by either increasing drag, or reducing drag. What is important is that a feedback signal, based on a building's sway, can change the drag according to feedback. The larger drag is used when the building is swaying into, meaning against, the wind's direction. The lesser drag is used when the building is swaying in the same direction as, and thus with the wind.

This brings us back to the adult pushing a child on a swing. When it is time to go back into the house or elsewhere, the adult merely switches the timing of the push forces. It's all in the timing. Nothing else really matters.

~~~~

"Grandpa," said Noah. "What you're proposing—wings on buildings that can be turned on and off—seems almost impossible. The timing has to be quick. Also, it takes energy to move something as big as a wing on a building, much less a bunch of wings."

"My dear grandson," I replied. "I wasn't born yesterday. I have proposed designs in my sketch pads that will do the trick. I keep my design sketches private for many reasons. For instance, I would jeopardize my future patent and/or proprietary rights by showing my sketches to others.

"Another reason why I don't show my designs to anybody walking by has to do with my time management. When people see something I have designed or proposed, a common response is, 'Why didn't you do it this other way?' People have ideas and suggestions all the time. If I stopped to listen to every suggestion, I'd spend my time doing only that and getting nothing else done. In my bicycle shop in Alton, Illinois, one thing is absent. There is no suggestion box.

"I am reminded of a story concerning Winston Churchill. In the 1930s when he was not in the majority in the House of Commons, he devoted much of his time to laying bricks—building a brick wall. Visitors coming to see Churchill invariably commented on his brick wall. It wasn't straight. It used bricks of the wrong color. The mortar was too thick or too thin. Churchill later wrote that nobody ever said that his brick wall was able to do everything that a brick wall needs to do. It was a brick wall.

"I don't show others my designs. The opinionated critics are prone to tell me what could be changed. They would do it such-and-such way. Fine. Let them come up with their own original designs. My designs are based on my extensive knowledge and understanding of structural control concepts.

"To this point, let me say that I don't need to supply energy, at least not energy from external sources. I would use fabrics, fabrics constrained in tracks or slides. Upon release based on a command, the fabric, or let's call it a sail, would unfurl itself using the energy available in the wind. I've stood on top of a tall building. The wind force is intense—and mostly vertical as the wind comes up the frontal face of the structure. The wind coming up the frontal face will unfurl and even lift the sail into place faster than you can say *Jackie Robinson*.

"I'll cite a second example as to how wind can lift objects. In Playa Del Rey, California, there is a park along the Pacific Ocean. The park has a tall cliff facing the water. Winds coming from the ocean are steady and strong. As the off-shore wind impacts the cliff, the wind is blocked by the cliff, thus rising vertically. A sport has developed called hang gliding. Enthusiasts run off the cliff (of course, with their hang gliders.) Yes, the hang gliders initially fall, but the skilled enthusiasts can navigate their hang gliders into a region of air with a strong uplift, also called an updraft. Lacking engines, the gliders continue to fall relative to the wind, but the wind rises faster upward than the relative fall or rate of descent.

This sport illustrates the simplicity of exploiting energy in the wind to lift objects. As I watched hang gliders, I felt at peace. God and large birds of prey know about this as well. Eagles can soar seemingly motionless for hours, remaining aloft with no exertion. They don't need to flap their wings. Instead they fly into and exploit an updraft.

"Wind represents what can be called a force field, a force field that can be taken advantage of. There are two types of force fields: conservative and non-conservative. Gravity is an example of a conservative force field. If you take an object, such as a brick, and move it up and down and sideways, upon returning to the original location no useful work has been extracted. In contrast, wind represents a non-conservative force field. You can move an object around in the wind, and come back to the starting point. If you have been clever, energy will be produced. This is why windmills work. We don't, in contrast, move bricks around in closed cyclical paths expecting to produce useful energy.

"The essence of mechanical engineering is based on two things: building engines that will create useful energy; and devices that allow for the transmission of energy. From a philosophical perspective, my suggested use of intelligent appendages, when incorporated onto structures subject to winds, boils down to engine building. I am able to capture and thus extract energy from the wind. Depending on a simple sign change, a change in timing, I can either add energy to a structure, or conversely dissipate energy from a structure. Of course, my objective is the latter. Work can only be obtained from non-conservative force fields. Nature gave us one, and it is handy and abundant—wind.

"When the sail of my appendage needs to be retracted, the wind itself will do that. I'll show you some of my sketches some day. My designs are lightweight, durable, and will even be relatively impervious to snow and ice formation. You see, in the old days, concrete and massive steel assemblies prevailed. A new era is dawning. Smart technology allows us to think outside of concrete boxes. Don't get fixated on concrete, and then pouring in more concrete if something wiggles. Noah, your decision to go into robotics and information technology should serve you well."

~~~~

In overview, the concept of *controllability* as introduced by Kalman [5] provides insight. I assert that torsional (twisting) vibrational modes are capable of being dissipated as well using feedback principles. Control of both cross-wind and torsional modes are best handled when the structure has been designed in advance for application of control systems theoretic principles.

I had arrived at designs for structural control using active aerodynamic appendages that operated inherently on the energy derived from the very wind itself, not from an external power source. Please allow my design implementation to utilize some modest electrical or energy source, such as for operation of sensors, logic devices, computers, switches, relays, and solenoids. When I speak of utilizing energy from the wind, I am referring to the energy needed to manipulate or actuate the appendage(s).

The designs that I envisioned would be lightweight and efficient. Several of my appendage designs incorporated inflatables like the ice removal devices on aircraft wings that function as inflatable boots. These function based on air pressure rather than moving parts. Moreover, the air flow required for the inflation and deflation was derived from the actual wind impacting the structure.

One of my other designs incorporated fabrics that unfurled and retracted based on captured wind. Growing up, I enjoyed sailing. My childhood home in Stratford, Connecticut, was close to where the Housatonic River flowed into Long Island Sound. Sailing had been a way of life for my family. Thus, I am fully aware of what it takes to have the wind catch and fill a sail. My sailing experiences inspired candidate designs for an aerodynamic appendage utilizing durable fabric sheets that would furl and unfurl themselves while capturing the wind's energy to cause the necessary cyclical change in appendage position. Per my designs, service and maintenance issues would be straightforward and minimal in implementation. My designs focused on low-tech, simplicity, minimal energy input, and ease of maintenance.

Another attribute of the aerodynamic appendage approach concerns the location where the stabilizing force is applied. Aerodynamic loading necessarily involves pressure changes distributed widely. Point loads are not involved or, at least, are minimal. It is seldom necessary to install significant additional bracing, as aerodynamic loads are inherently distributed to broad areas of a structure's exterior.

This attribute is in stark contrast to those damping systems that employ large reaction masses positioned on the upper levels of structures. As an example, the 1.2 million pounds of lead placed near the top of the John Hancock Tower in Boston required beefing up the structure's vertical load-bearing capability. Even the Harumi Island Triton Square Complex in Tokyo required the structures to be reinforced sufficiently to provide integrity for the point loadings.

When mass is added at the upper reaches of a structure, this additional mass loading requires yet more beefing up and thus yet more mass at the intermediate and lower levels. This all falls under the concept of the *premium for height*. Whenever mass is added to the upper portions of a structure, that involves the cost for that added mass plus the cost of bracing up the structure beneath to support it. To compound matters, the premium for height even impacts the foundation requirements. The laws of gravity are inviolate. Any mass added to a tall structure must be supported.

An economic point is reached where the cost of each additional floor, or mass placed near the top, isn't justified. This is very much the case when tuned mass damper (TMD) devices (tuned to damp or cancel a particular vibrational frequency) are installed, as the TMD devices are effective only at height where vibration is a problem. Nobody installs a TMD in the basement. Adding mass up top usually requires that additional bracing (and mass) be added at lower levels just to support that upper load.

The primary end of structural control, as I see it, is to bring a vibrating structure to rest, hence the vibrational energy goes to zero. To accomplish this, it is foundational that energy associated with vibrational sway needs to be dissipated. Some researchers and designers resorted to active control strategies wherein energy was used to create retarding forces. Some early research proposals to achieve sway control looked at the use of active tendons, tendons that would require external energy sources to generate pulling forces. As another example, the MTS Systems Corporation's TMD designs utilize hydraulic pumps to exert forces. The theory of tuned mass dampers falls under the category of passive devices. Because the MTS damping devices incorporated active hydraulic assist, the devices incorporated additional principles. Absent specifics, I was unable to ascertain the dynamics underlying the MTS system's operating principles.

Because the goal is to have zero vibrational energy, the way to achieve this is to remove or extract energy. Adding energy to a structure can only increase the total energy present. It is contrary to the aim of energy removal to pump additional energy into the building. Thus, using active devices, which consume energy to bring a structure to rest, would not be my advocated approach.

I strongly maintain that semi-active devices and strategies can accomplish the goal to remove energy from civil engineering structures. Semi-active devices have numerous advantages over active devices.

For those without a foundation in systems theory, a simple way to explain this might be to envision a gatekeeper. The person or entity who opens and closes a gate controls the passage through the gate but doesn't exert any pushing effort. That gatekeeper is a semi-active device. Semi-active devices require information to operate but not huge energy sources. In contrast, if a pump or piston pushes material through a gate or opening, that represents an active device. Active devices usually need two things: a command signal and an energy source to operate the pump or piston. Because the goal of structural control is energy dissipation from the structure, semi-active devices can accomplish such tasks without adding significant additional energy.

I will inject one more point about energy management in tall buildings. In a deflected structure, the stored potential energy is proportional to the deflection squared. Thus, if deflection is halved, then energy is cut by three-fourths. If peak sway amplitude can be reduced, it means that the energy has been reduced even more. This observation isn't vital to know, but knowing it makes me happier.

So there I was, holding a revolutionary theoretical concept in my hands—a metaphorical ball, if you will—a concept that could radically change the civil engineering profession, and the civil engineering industry didn't want to play with me.

Addressing Building Sway

Putting all these concepts together: aerodynamic drag forces, vibrational energy dissipation, and vortex shedding are all ingredients in a larger puzzle. It is possible to design smart appendages to address the issue of building sway mitigation. Solutions to the problem of building sway exist, but they can be very expensive if not designed in from the beginning. Said another way, the time to solve building sway should come before the design leaves the drawing board. Retrofitting a building after it has been erected isn't often feasible, and is costly if attempted.

Now I'd like to provide an example of how systems theoretic principles have been applied successfully in tall structure design.

In the 1980s, I served as a contributing author to Committee #36 of the Council on Tall Buildings and Urban Habitat, a non-profit organization that facilitates the exchange of knowledge on tall buildings around the world. The Council provides publications, research, working groups, and web resources. The committee's charge was to consider public perception and tolerance of structural motions. As such, I consider myself reasonably versed on these topics.

Several strategies can be implemented during the design and construction process to reduce building sway. One way to alleviate building sway in the cross-wind direction is through the successful use of feedback control principles, which require three things to be present:

- The structural vibration modes have adequate coupling between the cross-wind and along-wind directions. By proper building design this can be achieved. Notably, the desired coupling will occur if the structure's mass axis and the elastic axis are not collocated. Said in simpler terms, it behooves one to design a structure to be structurally asymmetric. See the work of Garland [13] for a clarification.
- A controlling force is available in the along-wind direction. This is usually straightforward given aerodynamic appendage control.
- The respective structural natural sway periods are sufficiently distinct, hence separated.

Of course, another strategy would be that the source for the excitation is eliminated or subdued. If vortex shedding is the source, confusing and disorganizing the vortex shedding represent potential options. If the vortex shedding can be defeated, then the cross-wind vibrational modes will be less excited.

The problem of aerodynamic excitation in structures is complex because wind commonly varies in its direction. Thus, the structural response can and will vary as the wind changes.

John Hancock Tower, photo courtesy of the Global Tall Building Database of the Council of Tall Buildings and Urban Housing

The John Hancock Tower in Boston was built having a thin profile. The building, sixty stories high, was based on a narrow trapezoidal footprint. In my mind, because of its thin profile it acted like a wing standing on edge and subject to lift. Like a wing in the stall position, in certain wind conditions the stall configuration created eddies that excited the structure's torsional modes. In my estimation, depending on the wind's direction, these torsional excitations were significant.

The retrofit remedy undertaken, contracted by MTS Systems Corporation of St. Paul, was to place two massive blocks of lead near the top. The lead blocks were supported by hydrostatic bearings, which permitted low-friction transverse sliding. The MTS dampers used hydraulics combined with nitrogen springs (akin to high pressure air bags) to allow the reaction masses to move horizontally relative to the structure. This retrofitted remedy, positioned on the 58th floor, was dubbed by MTS as tuned mass dampers (TMDs).

According to published literature, the two lead masses totaled 1.2 million pounds, 600,000 pounds in each of two blocks. With that much mass added near the top of the structure, the supporting vertical columns also needed to be reinforced as a retrofit. As an assumption, when a retrofit for additional vertical load carrying capacity was required, the logical place to install such reinforcing was within the elevator shaft confines.

It is, in most circumstances, folly to ask, "Can a given building be retrofitted?" The preferred approach is to design tall structures with intelligent systems in mind while the design is still on the drawing board to avoid expensive and inelegant solutions such as this.

Another point that I made in my early publications and at the 1991 ASCE Structures panel discussion was that adjacent structures should be designed in advance for implementation of control strategies. The success of the Triton Square design rests, to a large degree, in the differences in sway durations for each of the interconnected towers. Obviously, each of the towers was structurally reinforced internally to handle the point or concentrated horizontal loading.

In contrast, the now defunct Twin Towers of the World Trade Center were built to be identical twins.

Thus, each of the World Trade Center towers oscillated at the same fundamental sway period of approximately 11 seconds. The ability to interconnect these buildings for energy dissipation purposes was not feasible, even if any retrofit would ever have been contemplated.

Previously I have commented on the advantages, at least from the feedback control stabilization standpoint, of avoiding symmetry in construction. The work of Garland [13] made clear that the vibrational modes can be coupled if the mass axis and elastic axis of a structure are not collocated. The benefit of coupling of modes is that the control or dissipation of energy in any one mode will inherently cause all coupled modes to be controlled.

Resistance to My Theories

September 11, 2001, 9:03 a.m.: Flight 175 crashes at about 590 mph into the south face of the South Tower of the World Trade Center, between floors 77 and 85. All sixty-five people on board the aircraft die instantly on impact, and unknown hundreds in the building as well. Millions see the impact live. Parts of the plane, including the starboard engine, leave the building from its east and north sides, falling to the ground six blocks away. [4]

South Tower Victims

Only fourteen people escaped from the impact zone of the South Tower (floors 77 to 85) after it was struck by United Airlines Flight 175, and only four people from the floors above it. A few individuals escaped from as high up as the 84th floor using Stairwell A in the northwest corner, the only stairwell left intact after the impact. Investigators believe that Stairwell A remained passable until the South Tower collapsed at 9:59 a.m.

At or above the floors of impact in the South Tower, 614 people were killed. Only eighteen people are known to have escaped using Stairwell A before the South Tower collapsed; a further eleven people killed in the attacks are known to have been killed below the impact zone after United Airlines Flight 175 struck the South Tower.

~~~~

Noah then said, "Grandpa, it sounds like you had solutions to tall building stability problems."

"I had *theoretical* solutions to these issues," I replied. "I didn't have proven, tested solutions. There's a difference."

"But did you bring your ideas to civil engineers? It seems to me that they would be very interested."

I sighed. "I'm afraid you don't understand the culture of the civil engineering community. I believed in my theories. I still do. But testing them was another matter."

How to Test: Chicken vs. Egg

The steps I took to research structural sway were rather straightforward. I read the literature related to tall buildings. I explored ideas. I sought the aid of a colleague, Dr. Jim Stukel, who was on the faculty in the Department of Civil Engineering at the University of Illinois and had expertise in atmospheric air flow and turbulence. I also sought out Dr. Cris Cusano who assisted with computer simulation work.

While I felt right at home studying control of tall buildings, I was an outsider to the civil engineering community. My entry into control of structures was not based on any formal engraved invitation or welcome mat placed at the door. I simply invited myself into their midst like a party-crasher. To be frank, I wasn't received with open arms by the traditional structures people and civil engineers.

The papers by Klein [3] and then Klein, Cusano, and Stukel [1] appeared in 1971 and 1972, respectively. The response and reaction from the civil engineering community wasn't welcoming. This should have served as notice to me that I wasn't really appreciated by the civil engineering profession. Nonetheless, I fearlessly—perhaps even recklessly—charged onward.

~~~~

"Grandpa," said Noah. "I am confused about one thing—well, actually many things—but I'll bring up one now."

"Okay," I replied.

Noah continued, "If tall buildings have damping, at least a little, why don't they eventually settle down? In my mathematics classes the teachers introduced asymptotes. These are lines where wiggly and exponentially decaying motions will eventually settle down. Motion usually comes to rest. How is it possible that a tall building like the World Trade Center didn't settle down, but instead exhibited a sustained beat resonance? We saw that in the sway accelerometer recordings."

I explained, "A building acts like a giant capacitance. It has incoming energy. It also has a way to get rid of energy. Damping, such as friction, will turn the sway or movement energy into heat, thus making it go away.

"Everything boils down to what comes in, and what goes out or away. It's sort of like a bank account. Fluctuations are usually going on. Paychecks get deposited. We write checks so money goes out.

"In the case of buildings, the energy comes mostly from changes in wind pressures. The friction in the joints and some heating of beams dissipates or changes vibrational energy into heat. The degree or extent to which a building wiggles depends on the balance. If we could either increase the damping or get more energy out, the building's sway would lessen and even get close to the thing called an asymptote. Most steel-framed buildings have little damping. The damping has a hard time keeping up with the energy coming in. Wind is nasty as it varies, and can be self-generating. Flags flapping in the wind are examples. Vortex shedding is a pretty nasty source of wind energy because it has a dominant frequency. Whenever the vortex shedding frequency matches or is close to a structural frequency, we see a big-time problem. Another wind mechanism is called flutter. We don't see it in tall buildings much, but when a traffic sign on a steel post flops violently and twists back and forth—well, that is flutter. The Tacoma Narrows Bridge had a twisting problem. At first, motorists thought it was fun to drive across the bridge as it undulated and twisted, and nicknamed it Galloping Gertie. The oscillations grew until in November 1940, the bridge collapsed. A famous aerodynamic engineering expert, Dr. Theodore von Karman, diagnosed the problem. Swirling eddies caused differences in air pressures between the top and bottom of the bridge's deck. The solution was simple—add metal grating. The air openings in the deck alleviate any pressure differences. That is why many bridge roadway surfaces today are constructed with metal grating. Come to think of it, we could solve most building sway problems by eliminating cladding. The wind could just blow through the work areas. Unfortunately, not too many renters would want to expose their employees to wind, rain, and snow.

"The energy coming into a structure is hard to control or stop. I have long advocated alternatives to get rid of excessive energy in structures. I have looked at two options: (1) increasing energy dissipation, and (2) devising smart strategies to eliminate or slow the energy coming in. Most of my efforts were focused on the former, increasing a structure's ability to get rid of energy. A third option is to add bracing and thereby stiffen the structure. That approach might look attractive, but it has many drawbacks. Stiffening a building is like tightening a violin string. The string still vibrates but now at a higher pitch. Oddly, increasing the pitch or natural frequency does not lessen the peak acceleration felt by the occupant. Instead, it makes the vibration more noticeable. I seldom advocate the third approach.

"Let's consider the first option of getting rid of energy. Friction and even viscous-elastic dampers work in proportion to the amount of motion present. In general, dampers and friction cease being as effective as amplitudes become lower. In stark contrast, if we can find a damping device or mechanism that keeps on damping regardless of amplitudes, all sorts of good things happen. The motion will mimic that of a brick sliding on a flat surface. Dry or sliding friction, also known as Coulomb friction, maintains its full force so long as any sliding occurs. That is why things with dry friction come to rest, sometimes abruptly.

"My advocated appendage feedback designs behave like dry bricks. A tall structure that has aerodynamic appendages can cause the motion to come to a complete stop, or at least drastically diminish the sway amplitudes. The results in my 1972 ASME paper [1] showed that motion was reduced by about 75 percent."

"Grandpa," said Noah. "I'm anxious to hear more. Let's move on."

~~~~

In the world of civil engineering, to establish or prove a point one must get access to a building and implement the innovation. For me, that objection became a chicken and egg problem. Only theories that are proven can be put into practice, and yet one can't prove success in a real building without having a building designed incorporating a given feature.

In my early papers, I didn't make outrageous claims. The title of my 1972 American Society of Mechanical Engineers (ASME) paper [1] read simply as "Investigation of a Method to Stabilize Wind Induced Oscillations in Large Structures." By using the word "investigation," I emphasized that my paper wasn't the complete answer and that I hadn't demonstrated the concept at so-and-so building at XYZ Street. Rather, I was investigating a method, essentially a theoretical idea.

From my perspective, the task of the validation of structural control was horrendous and insurmountable. Tall buildings are typically located in densely crowded cities where the city enforces strict building codes. This raises the issue of compliance with building codes. It is unreasonable to expect that the City of New York, for example, would waive its building codes to permit the conduct of an experiment.

One can't prove a hypothetical concept applicable to a large structure unless one either personally owns a large structure or receives an invitation to perform modifications to somebody else's building. Being able to enter a public building with the stated intent to record its movement is customarily denied. Even if I could gain access to a structure for an experiment, city codes and fire department inspectors must also go along with it. Furthermore, the media would certainly take notice if wings or sails were attached to a building as an experiment.

Modifying an existing building to conduct an experiment is likewise frowned upon. Any of the governing parties can object. Most persons and institutions who invest in a major building construction project are already wealthy, and their goal is to preserve and protect their amassed fortune. These investors are not interested in taking unnecessary risks based on some new, unproven, theoretical idea. A single objection becomes the deal-breaker.

In my situation, I could do conceptual research and publish papers based on mathematics and computer simulations, but the critics rejected my work because it wasn't proven to their satisfaction and because it went counter to their prevailing ways of thinking. Traditional civil engineers prefer to pour in more concrete or make a structure stiffer if something might wiggle. Comparing a tall, cantilevered structure to a flexing or bending aircraft wing doesn't go along with their culture and mindset. Even discussion of such silly notions makes them uneasy.

Yet another complication rests with the matter of wind tunnel testing. Wind tunnels replicate the Earth's boundary layer. The most prominent wind tunnel is operated at the University of Western Ontario. Wind tunnel testing is both complex and expensive. The success of a scale model through a wind tunnel test is required before anyone will build a full sized, state-of-the-art structure.

The entire premise of wind tunnel testing with a scale model depends upon preservation of what are called dimensionless (or non-dimensional) numbers. Dimensionless numbers don't have units and are often obtained as ratios of quantities that have dimensions, but whose dimensions cancel out in the mathematical operation. For example, alcohol by volume, which characterizes the concentration of ethanol in an alcoholic beverage, could be written as mL / 100 mL. Since both parts of the ratio have the same unit (mL), the units cancel each other out, and the result is a dimensionless number. The Mach number and the Reynold's number are a few other examples. Prior to the wonders of the modern high-speed digital computer, scientists, engineers, and mathematicians had to be far more cunning and clever. Dimensionless numbers permitted considerable insight.

The science of scale model testing does not normally allow for a compliant dynamic structure, and the necessary dimensionless numbers become too unwieldly to manage. Therefore, the ability to test some proposed control concept isn't technically feasible. Unfortunately, the requirement for scale model testing remains as a prerequisite before any contemplated structure can get the approval of building plans by the city's building code commission or authorities. Without that approval, no city will permit construction of any new skyscraper. Just the writing of building codes is costly; therefore, many cities merely borrow codes already written by other cities.

City building codes are far from perfect. But the practice has been established that wind tunnel testing of scale models must be performed. There are just a handful of facilities worldwide that perform such tests, so any new proposed structural design must be contracted for study by one of those facilities.

My Paper Goes into Limbo

After presenting "Investigation of a Method to Stabilize Wind Induced Oscillations in Large Structures," I submitted the paper to *ASME Transactions*, but all the returned peer reviews were at extreme and opposing ends of the spectrum. The editors at *ASME* were uncertain what to do with such polarized reviews. Reviewers who were mechanical engineering types were favorably impressed with the paper and recommended it be published. On the contrary, the traditional civil engineering types were characteristically indignant. They declared the paper to be pointless and unworthy of publication. One reviewer labelled me as unqualified and another cited my improper use of a linear model. My modelling used a linear tenth order model for structural sway, whereas the dissenting reviewer claimed I was off base as nonlinear models apply. To that point, the objective of the 1972 ASME paper was to arrive at methods to dissipate energy from swaying structures. Frankly, the model used to represent the structure, whether linear or nonlinear, does not alter the fact that if a smart force opposes motion then energy will be dissipated.

When editors get mixed reviews on a paper being considered for publication, it is common that the paper gets sent out for additional reviews. The Klein, Cusano, and Stukel paper [1] went through several review cycles. Instead of resolving the bipolar problem, the problem persisted. And so the editors rejected my paper for consideration in the *ASME Transactions*. The problem of rewriting the paper to satisfy the dissenting reviewers fell back onto me. Eventually, I set the paper aside to work on things with greater likelihood of success.

The 1972 ASME paper [1] represents an oddity of sorts. Copies could be ordered, for a modest fee, from *ASME* for an eighteen-month window following its 1972 publication. The paper was not published in an archival journal, something that is permanent and available in libraries worldwide. Instead, it was published as a pamphlet paper.

As possibly the earliest paper on building stabilization using control theoretic principles, many researchers and authors thereafter addressing the topic cited Klein, Cusano, and Stukel [1]. The rub was that many of those authors had never read the paper. They cited it based on previous citations because some other author or authors before them cited the paper. The motivation to cite my paper was obvious since it was the first paper to suggest that a tall civil engineering structure was a candidate for active feedback control.

Furthermore, two typographical errors got mixed in along the way. One citing author misspelled Stukel's last name; an inadvertent *c* got mixed in so "Stukel" became "Stuckel." A second error was that the citation number "72-WA/Aut-11" was inadvertently typed as "72-WA/Aut-H." (The citation number is shorthand for "Winter Annual Meeting, Automatic Control Division, Paper #11." I attended that meeting, held in New York City, and presented the paper to an audience of attendees.) The *11* was typed or read incorrectly along the way and became *H*. Because of these two typographical markers, I can usually tell if a citing author has read my paper or if the author cited it based on some previous citing.

Because the 1972 ASME paper appeared only in pamphlet form, the paper stands in an area of limbo. Though it has been cited hundreds of times by other authors, very few people have ever actually read the paper. Moreover, any new researcher coming upon the citation is stuck in a dead end. That researcher has no practical means to access or obtain a copy of the paper, except for possibly communicating with me to request a copy for personal use (per fair use terminology).

Opposing Research Appears

After the semi-publication of my ASME paper in 1972, two dissenting papers appeared in civil engineering literature, one from Abdul-Rohman [14] and another from Soong [15]. Both authors conducted scale model tests involving active aerodynamic appendage control. Both authors made basic assumptions—wrong in my opinion— and both went on to suggest that the use of active appendages would not be feasible in practice, or would only be of limited utility. Abdul-Rohman and Soong assumed that:

- The appendage would be positioned to be an upward vertical extension of the structure and that it would be centered on the top of the structure.
- They never considered drag coefficient changes, but instead looked at changes in projected cross-sectional or projected frontal area.
- The physical size of the required appendages would be

mammoth (Abdul-Rohman, for example, assumed fifteen percent added projected frontal area on top of the structure.)
- The power to flip or manipulate the appendage would be excessive.
- The timing and synchronization required would be difficult to achieve and sluggish at best.
- My approach of a nonlinear "bang-bang" or "on-off" controller wasn't *optimal.*

I strongly argue against the above assumptions. Because the placement of the appendage was centered on top of the scale-model structure in their respective experimental studies, appendage control would have only minimal effectiveness. The region of turbulent and low velocity air directly above the structure tends to be inconsequential aerodynamically. The bulk of the slip stream or air rush is directed upwards along the frontal face of the building. Certainly, experiments with an improper placement of the appendage will fail to give positive results. No attempt was made to place manipulated appendages along the leading edges.

The paper by Abdul-Rohman [14] was reviewed by and appeared in *ASCE Transactions.* From my perspective, it was improper that the Abdul-Rohman paper discredited my prior work and ideas while my attempts to publish in *ASCE Transactions* were rejected. Moreover, the editors accepting the Abdul-Rohman paper were strongly critical of my work and never afforded me the opportunity to review the paper or to respond in any manner prior to its publication. My first knowledge of the dissenting papers came only upon reading them in print, post-review and post-publication. In my mind, I was engaged on a playing field far from level.

Note that the title of the paper by Soong [15] was "Active Structural Control Theory and Practice." Soong's title suggests the definitive answers to virtually all issues related to active structural control. The title of the Abdul-Rohman paper [14] was "Optimal Control of Tall Buildings by Appendages." The inferences respectively were that both papers, by Soong and Abdul-Rohman, embodied the latest word on such a mathematically rich topic and application: optimal control of a structure. In truth, the understanding of optimal control principles in both papers fell short.

My designs as proposed, specifically the active aerodynamic appendages, would operate using *time-optimal* strategies. Time-optimal feedback systems are also referred to as "bang-bang" and "on-off." The control logic for time-optimal control is little more than an on-off switching action. Time-optimal is based on Pontryagin's Maximum Principle [16], at times also referred to as Pontryagin's Minimum Principle. (Recall that mathematicians can insert a sign change at will, so the maximum and minimum issues are just mirror reflections of each other. They are mathematical equivalents.)

In simple language, *time-optimal* implies a simple binary operation. The alternating maximum and minimum usage of the control action allows the system being controlled to achieve its goal in minimum time. The essence of *time-optimal control* is to cause some desired outcome to occur in the smallest amount of time. Think of a race car going from Point A to Point B in minimum time. Assume traveling on a highway with no other traffic and no speed limits or restrictions. Assume also that the objective is to arrive at Point B while coming to a full stop. The time-optimal control strategy is simple. Start at Point A with full throttle. Speed will increase to reach its maximum. At a precise switching point, one reverses the control action by letting off the accelerator and applying full braking action. If the driver has switched from full throttle to full braking at the precise right moment, the vehicle will come to a stop at Point B in minimum time. All other strategies of usage of throttle and braking will consume a greater elapsed time. Therefore, all or nothing is time-optimal.

The definition of *optimal*, as used by both Abdul-Rohman and Soong, was based on *linear-quadratic-regulator* LQR theory [17], something quite elegant in one sense but unnecessary, overly restrictive, and even inappropriate for structural smart appendage control. A linear or proportional feedback control is a modulated and weaker control, therefore inappropriate in the application to achieve structural damping. Those who advocate LQR designs for structural control are, simply put, unqualified and misinformed. The LQR assumptions and restrictions have little bearing on the task of dissipating unwanted vibrational energy from a structure, at least in cases where wind energy as a control force is free and available. To achieve structural control, the objective should be to maximize structural damping—that is, energy dissipation. It is sub-optimal to use less available control action than the available maximum and minimum. Therefore, the experiments of Abdul-Rohman and Soong yielded substandard results.

Optimal is a delicate concept because something can't be optimal until and unless a definition is first provided. There must be a criterion specified to define optimal. Moreover, all sorts of definitions can be used, so one must be careful to not mix apples with oranges.

Under my assumptions, the problem is best viewed and approached using time-optimal principles rather than LQR principles. I apologize to my reader, but once arguments were raised, the battle ensued. The topics of optimal control and time-optimal control are advanced topics in control systems theory. Volumes are available to any who wish to read more. Note that [16] and [17] represent suitable introductory points. Unfortunately, the subject matter of optimal control is demanding. I feel compelled to provide references as the dissenting authors opted to take up that battle. It was civil engineers such as Abdul-Rohman and Soong, supported by *ASCE Transactions* editors and reviewers, who threw down the gauntlet before me. In my view, there is little wonder that the civil engineering profession rejected the feasibility of aerodynamic appendage control given *ASCE Transactions* and other papers describing experiments that came up with negative and/or marginal findings. However, had they truly attempted to understand my proposed solution, they would have seen the fallacies of each of their assumptions listed above and the viability of my solution: simply, to use the wind (force) itself to control lightweight appendages on leading edges of a tall structure and thus to dissipate energy, i.e. semi-active intelligent aerodynamic appendages.

Trying to Get Data

I was at a disadvantage in responding to published papers that presented opposing conclusions to my papers, as the authors refused to disclose the data supporting their claims.

I deeply respect capitalism and the right of any person or corporation to maintain trade secrets. But during my decades of interactions with the civil engineering profession, I encountered a roadblock. Reviewers who recommended that my manuscripts be rejected at times stated the following reason: the work submitted by Klein is pointless because the problem has already been solved. Then the dissenting reviewer(s) would cite or infer some previously published paper(s), obviously extant in the civil engineering literature.

Authors, such as Mahmoodi *et al* [18], associated with the World Trade Center and the 3M Company, made claims in published scholarly papers, but they refused to disclose the data to support their claims and conclusions. The scientific method is clear: If a conclusion or finding is made in a scholarly publication, the data must be presented or made accessible to permit independent researchers to validate the findings. I once approached Mahmoodi for access to the data that would support his published damper performance claim. He was at a trade show representing 3M Company products, notably the dampers used in the World Trade Center. Although a friendly guy, he was evasive in responding to my request.

Mahmoodi first stated that the data was proprietary. He then proceeded to get out some strip chart recordings of World Trade Center accelerometer data. However, before he showed me the recording, he covered up all data except for a short strip. Moreover, the portion he showed me did not have the scale or order of magnitudes of the respective axes. What he showed me was a single beat resonance. As a systems vibration theorist, I was familiar with beat resonance. Many years prior to my interchange with Mahmoodi, Fred Chang, the structural engineer for the World Trade Center, had shown me similar accelerometer records. I was also familiar with beat resonance in structures from my work as contributing author to Committee #36 of the Council on Tall Buildings and Urban Habitat. Because the accelerometer records Chang showed me in 1975 were not public, I simply observed what Mahmoodi showed me, not revealing that I had other sources.

Beat resonance is like the sound of a twin-engine airplane in flight. If the two engines are close in RPM (speed) but still off slightly, the bystander on the ground or the passenger hears a sound that grows, peaks, and diminishes. This repeats and is referred to as a beat resonance. The pilot can usually adjust the engine speeds to cause the beat to go away so that they sound steady, as if there were only one engine.

Structures commonly exhibit beat resonance. The condition arises when two natural frequencies are close to each other. Recall that structures can oscillate in cross directions and torsionally. If two frequencies are close to each other, beat resonance can occur. Unlike airplane engines, the frequencies associated with a structure can't be easily changed.

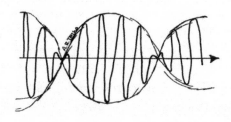

The diagram above illustrates a process with a resonant beat phenomenon. Time advances to the right as indicated by the arrow. The diagram is presented to illustrate a generic resonant beat, not to show or represent World Trade Center data. In the case of the World Trade Center, the fundamental period was approximately eleven seconds. The much longer beat envelope enclosing the dominant harmonic was several minutes in duration.

Mahmoodi showed me only the portion for the World Trade Center recording of a single beat envelope. He then made a patently absurd statement by saying that the proof of the 3M damper effectiveness was represented in how a wind gust hit the building, causing it to sway, then the sway diminished because of the action of the 3M dampers.

At that point I knew Mahmoodi was grossly misinformed or had scant understanding of structural motion or was living in a delusional world. In my view, Mahmoodi was not qualified to be in charge of damping hardware designs for tall structures. The presence of a beat resonance in a structure does not constitute proof as to the effectiveness of the damping. Instead, the presence of the beat resonance suggests the ineffectiveness of the dampers.

Unable to Collaborate or Test

Another problem facing me was more philosophical in nature. I would like to think that conceptual and theoretical proposals and options should be discussed and explored. The goal of the advancement of knowledge should rest on an examination of a myriad of competing ideas. In my view, it was a breach of the scientific method to say, as *ASCE Transactions* editors told me, that alternative approaches were not publishable as one solution or remedy was in hand. I see no harm in a scholarly profession having a diversity of problem-solving remedies and approaches as opposed to a fixation on just one, with an *a priori* rejection of differing ideas. The civil engineering community appeared, at least to me, to be content having just one approach to addressing problems and rejected other candidate ideas by claiming that one remedy existed. I considered the few remedies in place as not validated.

Upon reflection, my decades of interactions with the structural control problem boiled down to researching alternative ways to view and potentially address structural sway problems. A foundational principle of feedback systems theory is that the dynamic properties of what is commonly called the plant (in our case, the tall building) can be altered not only by brute force modifications and/or physical changes to the plant, but also by feedback loop placement(s) external to the plant. Examples of the former would be the installation of dampers or additional bracing. In the situation of the WTC, the proposed remedy involved retrofitting of 20,000 dampers. Examples of the latter include the innovative use of feedback principles where information is manipulated and used to command an available input and/or an internal parameter. As an example of the latter, a hydraulic damper can be altered by adjusting a valve setting. Fly-by-wire is the basis of how modern aircraft, for example, often use electronics, hydraulics, and compensation techniques. The addition or change within a logic system has the potential to alter, and hence 'shape,' the plant's dynamics.

~~~~

"Grandpa," said Noah with a puzzled look. "Sometimes you say really odd things. For example, you just said that you can shape a plant's dynamics. Why did you say 'shape' but not something like alter, improve, or change? How can something that moves have its shape changed?"

"Noah," I said. "Remember that I live within a black hole. I speak a different language.

"I will tell you about my usage of the word 'shape.' Within the feedback control systems culture, the practitioners commonly refer to the *time domain* and the *frequency domain*. For one fluent in the art of feedback control, the conversion or translation from one domain to the other—the time domain to the frequency domain and the converse—and the symbology needs no explanation. In the frequency domain, typically on a Bode plot using logarithmic axes of amplitude and frequency, the character of a plant can be embodied in the shape of the plotted curve. To say that we *shape* a dynamic system implies that we are changing its graphical shape on a frequency response plot. Most commonly, the frequency response of a plant is plotted using log-log coordinates. The engineer at Bell Laboratories who popularized this was Hendrik W. Bode (1905-1982), therefore the plots are commonly referred to as Bode plots. The dynamic behavior of the plant is evident in the graphical shape of a curve. This leads me to yet another term, *compensator*, also called an *equalizer*. The equalizer represents the log-log plot of what is inserted in series with the log-log plot of the plant. When the two plots are combined or superimposed, the result is the compensated plant. What was added caused the summation to be equal to what we wanted. Hence, the word 'equalizer.' As a last point on language usage, the equalizer and the plant are usually in series and get multiplied. When plotted on a log axis, multiplication is reduced to addition and/or subtraction. The whole purpose of feedback systems is to make problem-solving simple. In the log-log frequency domain, the task boils down to simple addition and subtraction of graphed plots. This might sound confusing, but to a practitioner, it is as basic as 2 plus 2 equals 4.

"To shape a system dynamically means to cause its dynamic response to be as we so desire it to be."

"Grandpa, now that makes sense," said Noah. "You're using words related to frequencies, such as bandwidth. I now realize that you are fluent in things being described by radio terminology."

He paused.

To follow this discussion about the insights gained from thinking in terms related to frequencies, I went on, "Noah, by now you should understand that steel-framed tall buildings share many common attributes with musical instruments, such as the tendency to resonate. The use of musical terms brings clarity as we discuss tall building issues."

~~~~

The approach of the feedback control systems theoretician is to shape a system's dynamic behavior by manipulating some signal when it is at a low energy level.

A second instance concerning a claim in a scholarly paper and proprietary rights was during an interaction with a former classmate and friend, Niel R. Petersen, from our days together at Grandview University in Des Moines in the late 1950s. Petersen [19] authored a paper dealing with the MTS Systems Corporation's Tuned Mass Dampers (TMD) in the Citicorp Center in New York. Petersen was also instrumental in the MTS retrofit in the John Hancock Tower in Boston, Massachusetts. MTS opted to publish its findings on the Citicorp Center.

A TMD creates a zero or cancelling effect at one frequency, but in doing so the order of the system is increased by two (because of the addition of an extra degree of freedom). As you recall from my previous discussion, it is called a tuned mass damper specifically because it is tuned to damp (or cancel) a particular vibrational frequency and only that frequency (at least within a narrow frequency band). The traditional

TMD will cause the structure's excitation at the tuned frequency to be nulled. But a by-product is that the original system acquires an additional natural frequency.

I am familiar with the theory and practice of tuned mass dampers since they are classic textbook material in my discipline. However, the textbook TMD is passive, whereas the MTS system is active because it employs hydraulic actuators. The MTS design used nitrogen springs along with active hydraulic assist.

I am not alleging an error, but I am explaining how I wanted to validate the findings and conclusions in Petersen's paper [19]. Without knowledge of the dynamics internal to the TMD, within its metaphorical black box, I was unable to validate Petersen's performance claims because they didn't make total sense to me.

While at a Structures Congress in Boston, I asked Niel Petersen some pointed questions. One question was for him to provide the mathematics of the feedback logic that commanded the system's hydraulic actuators. His reply was, "Sorry, the details of the MTS design are proprietary."

Please bear in mind, I've already stated that I acknowledge and respect intellectual property rights. I completely appreciate a company's right to retain its product design information as proprietary. My problem was that two companies, 3M Company and MTS Corporation, had published findings in papers that bore scholarly weight. Moreover, editors—including those of *ASCE Transactions*—rejected my submissions, claiming the problems were already solved. I deemed the stated solutions as flawed or at least not validated, and without the audit trail including the data, I was unable to refute the editors' rejections of my submissions.

I considered the ethics and judgments of the editors to be seriously flawed. The two papers I have cited were written by authors in the employ of companies marketing proprietary products. Claims as to product performance were made, yet the data to validate the claims were withheld. Both papers promoted applications at specific commercial locations. The crowning insult was to be told that the scholarly society had no interest in any discussion of alternative or competing ideas.

What normally happens (or *should* happen in the scholarly world) is that when an error or unsupported published claim is alleged, then some form of correspondence can be submitted to the editors for consideration and possible publication. Of course, the original author is afforded the opportunity to respond in the format of the journal or publication. Scholarly integrity must be the foundation of the scientific method.

If a corporation wants to make product-related performance claims, fine. But these claims can be stated in paid advertisements on highway billboards or commercials.

The two papers I have cited even went to the point of identifying the buildings involved. If I had approached the authors or building owners to enter these buildings and take my own measurements, I surely would have been denied access.

I advocate that society is better served when multiple means to address problems are made available or, at minimum, are discussed. This includes, of course, the forum to bring ideas forward and present them for consideration. I have long advocated that feedback theoretic principles have applicability as to the problem of structural sway control. Many practitioners in civil and structural engineering clearly didn't share or embrace such views. Instead of entering a discussion of the merits of competing ideas, the opposing side dismissed the ideas *a priori* as being unworthy of discussion.

Theories Are Just Theories

To date, some of my structural control ideas have been put into practice, whereas others, notably active intelligent aerodynamic appendages, remain untried. The active aerodynamic appendage concept is still but a theory. I am a realist, as I fully understand the immense challenges and unknowns.

Theories are called theories because that's all they are—just theories.

Nonetheless, I have confidence that the potential exists, but only as a theory as of this writing. Those authors who have conducted and reported on scale model tests on appendage control typically adopted assumptions and configurations that I would avoid. Because said authors never made adequate contact with me, I was not able to provide guidance and counsel.

I see little point in responding to the allegations that appendage control had other limitations. The dissenters of my work never even once communicated with me to clarify their distinctly inadequate grasp of system theoretic principles and my proposed ideas. Their conclusions stemmed from assumed hardware configurations, configurations of their own invention. My papers have never provided design specifications but rather theoretical concepts. Their understanding of feedback control theoretic principles was lacking at best.

As a point of clarification, I did visit with Dr. T.T. "Larry" Soong on July 9, 1974. I know the exact date because I was active as a private pilot. I recorded all flights in my pilot log, which includes airports and dates. I traveled to see Dr. Soong in my private airplane, and I toured his laboratory at the University of Buffalo in Buffalo, New York. However, I was not afforded an opportunity to critique his later publication [15] nor have any input prior to its publication.

This flight log shows my trip to Buffalo, New York.

Perhaps if I'd been allowed the opportunity to collaborate on testing my theories, they could have become more than just theories.

My Interest in Structural Control Is Rekindled

By 1983, my interest in research on structures was waning. At that time, my research interests had turned to bicycles. However, on September 19, 1985, a devastating earthquake hit Mexico City. This renewed my interests in structures and structural control. I attended several meetings and symposia devoted to the post-Mexico City earthquake topic. That resurgence lasted for several years, but then faded into obscurity. I became involved intellectually but didn't publish my research ideas.

An earthquake of 5.3 magnitude hit Mexico City. All earthquakes are harmful, but the Mexico City earthquake was amplified because of geological conditions. Due to the nature of the earthquake and the fact that Mexico City was situated on a former lake bed, the effects of the tremor was devastating. The former lake bed had filled in with silt and sand over the past thousand years or so. As such, the foundation supporting Mexico City shook, amplifying the quake like a bowl of soup being agitated side to side. The supporting soil essentially turned to a liquid as the agitation dislodged the silt and sand particles. Because of the liquefaction of the supporting soil, some buildings sank into the soft ground.

Strangely, only about one percent of the city's buildings failed, but these were the buildings most vital in terms of providing public services. Hospitals, police stations, communication centers, and similar public buildings were in the affected height range—about six to ten stories high. That height range yielded a natural sway period that coincided with the earthquake's sway period. As I recall, the peak-to-peak horizontal movement at ground level was approximately three feet (roughly one meter).

One cause of building failure resulted because of hammering. Consider, for example, two adjacent buildings of ten and twenty stories respectively. The shorter building would sway excessively because of the match in frequencies. On the other hand, the taller building would be relatively immune to excessive sway. Being longer in duration, the sway period of the taller building wasn't excited nearly as much. The hammering resulted because the excessive sway of the shorter structure caused collisions with the taller adjacent building.

In the period following the Mexico City earthquake, I came up with design and energy dissipation remedies—at least conceptually. It was vividly clear to me that active systems where external power would be required are pointless. It just isn't practical to have engines running and actuators ready for hundreds of years in anticipation of the next quake. Aerodynamic approaches would be pointless as well.

Instead, I envisioned a solution applicable to adjacent structures. My idea was that structures would exhibit different sway periods. My conceptual remedy involved metal cutting as a form of energy dissipation. Metal cutting can be easily accomplished by utilizing the dissimilar sway periods of adjacent structures. No power source is required. The combination of a cutting tool striking into an adjoining workpiece can remain in place for centuries. The energy can be dissipated efficiently should relative movement ever occur, such as when an earthquake happens.

Metal cutting has distinct advantages. Energy is dissipated and doesn't rebound. When a metal cutting tool moves through a workpiece, the shearing and deformation produces chips. The chips are heated as energy is dissipated as heat. The force required to cut metal, based on controlled shearing, is constant and independent of velocity. Moreover, if any metal is cut away following a quake, the workpiece can be easily replaced. I consider my design implementations as proprietary. Pleck,

Metz, and Conry [20] provide some overview of metal cutting as an energy management mechanism.

My renewed interest in structural control was to continue for many more decades.

My Firsthand Look

September 11, 2001, 9:29 a.m.: President Bush makes his first public statements about the attacks. "Today, we've had a national tragedy," he starts. "Two airplanes... have crashed... into the World Trade Center... in an apparent terrorist attack on our country," and leads a moment of silence. [4]

Honoring the Heroes

Firefighters across the country honor the 343 firefighters who died in the World Trade Center tragedy by climbing the equivalent of 110 flights of stairs—the number of stories in each of the twin towers. In Colorado, firefighters march up the Manitou Incline hiking trail, which reaches an elevation of 2,000 feet. In San Antonio, emergency responders, including police officers and firefighters in full gear, climb the Tower of the Americas building twice to honor the fallen heroes of 9/11. Others complete the climb in stair-steppers in gyms and fitness centers across the United States. Many of these climbs are held as annual events to keep the memory of the fallen heroes alive.

~~~~

"Your theory for solving the wind-induced sway problem sounds pretty good to me," Noah said. "It's a shame you never got to test it."

My grandson was starting to see how I felt about the whole thing. While I didn't mean to bring him down, it was at least heartening to know he understood.

"So how does this fit in with the World Trade Center towers?" Noah continued. "Since your theories were never tested, I assume they were never put into practice. And I don't recall ever seeing one of your appendages on top of the towers. I assume since the towers were tall structures, they had sway issues. So the sway issues must have been solved another way, right?"

"That's correct, Noah," I replied. "The World Trade Center towers had sway issues just like many other steel-framed tall structures. Some tall steel-framed structures weren't adequately designed with sway in mind. One case in point was the John Hancock Tower in Boston. Both the John Hancock Tower and the WTC underwent post-construction retrofitting."

"And how do you know all this?" he asked.

"Because I read published reports. I attended symposia where retrofitting approaches were formally presented. I also spoke personally with the company representatives who performed the retrofit. In the case of the Twin Towers, I also saw and inspected a typical damper firsthand."

Wind-Induced Sway Problems with the North Tower

In March 1975, a story appeared in *The Wall Street Journal* concerning an elevator failure in the World Trade Center. The front-page article reported on a breakaway elevator incident involving an elevator car that reportedly experienced a freefall for some distance. As I recall, it was a hundred feet or more. Fortunately, a braking safety mechanism arrested the freefalling elevator car, and no lives were lost. My understanding was that the failure involved an express elevator that was suspended from the Sky Lobby on the 78th floor in the North Tower. This incident put into motion other events that involved me professionally.

I later determined that this incident initiated some investigations of the World Trade Center regarding alleged structural sway. The concern was that structural sway had affected the integrity of the elevator suspension cable, the elevator car, and the hoist system. Some tests were performed. Building sway was measured based on accelerometer recordings. A little more than nine months later, I was shown these accelerometer recordings. The recordings that I later saw were dated March 19, 1975, shortly following the elevator failure incident. As the story of my interaction with the WTC unfolds, I will return to the significance of the March 1975 elevator incident.

A Real-Life Problem to Test My Theories

My wife Marjorie, daughter Victoria, and I traveled east on a Christmas holiday trip. As a fledgling private pilot, I flew into Albany, New York, on Monday, December 22, 1975. At the time, my family and I were combining my scheduled visit to the World Trade Center with a visit to my wife's sister and brother-in-law in Albany.

My flight log shows me flying into Albany, New York on Monday, December 22, 1975.

As mentioned in Part 1, I had scheduled to meet the following day with representatives of the firm responsible for the structural engineering of the World Trade Center, the prominent engineering firm of Worthington, Skilling, Helle & Jackson.

On Tuesday morning, I took the New York Central train from Albany to New York City for a day trip. Having lived in Connecticut during my childhood, I was familiar with taking a train into New York City. Upon my arrival in New York, I took a subway to the financial district. I exited from the subway and walked to the North Tower. The weather was the typically brisk weather of a winter in New York.

I met by appointment in the early afternoon with Fred Chang, a Professional Engineer (PE) and one of the World Trade Center's structural engineers. Chang's office was in the North Tower, located on the 34th floor, according to my recollections. At the time, both World Trade Center towers had been erected and completed on the exterior. By then, the North Tower had been completed and was fully occupied. Certain upper floors of the South Tower were undergoing some interior construction, but most of the lower floors were finished and occupied.

Following the usual niceties, Fred Chang pulled out some strip chart recordings. The recordings were of accelerometer measurements taken in the North Tower.

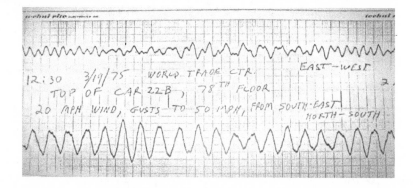

The strip chart recordings were revealing. The lateral North-South (N-S) and East-West (E-W) accelerations were recorded on the top of an elevator car positioned at the 78th floor. The bottom (lower) record of the N-S directional accelerations indicated two dominant characteristics: (1) the eleven-second period of what was obviously the fundamental or first harmonic mode of translational vibration, and (2) the presence of what is called a beat phenomenon or alternatively a beat resonance, something common in structures. This beat resonance occurs when two vibrational frequencies are relatively close to each other. It is also common that vibrational modes will be coupled, although to varying degrees. The excitation of one mode will in turn commonly excite other modes through the coupling mechanism. See Garland [13] for a more detailed explanation of these concepts.

The E-W accelerometer recordings (in the upper strip) revealed a secondary E-W sway with a period of approximately five seconds. The upper recording (above) of the East-West direction of acceleration was more confusing and contained multiple frequencies. One period present was the eleven-second period duration, thus the same as the first or fundamental mode. Superimposed on that first mode was a five-second period vibration. I assumed that the five-second period vibration was associated with, and thus excited by, vortex shedding. Absent additional records, such as from some other location, I was not able to tie that five-second period to the second translational mode.

My knowledge of the accelerometer data was helpful as I later became involved with other World Trade Center issues. It was my observation of the accelerometer recordings that allowed me to have specific knowledge of the respective N-S and E-W sway periods for the North Tower. I assumed that the South Tower had similar dynamic characteristics, since both towers shared a common structural plan.

Chang went on to explain the significance of the recordings. Because of my prior reading of news articles about tall building sway issues, I was aware that the accelerometer recordings were taken as related to the errant elevator incident in March of 1975. The strip chart recordings also included handwritten notes as to prevailing wind direction and speed. I asked Chang how the wind external to the building was known or measured. Chang replied that the wind information was obtained from the Newark, New Jersey, airport as publicly reported, which wasn't far across the Hudson River from the lower Manhattan financial district. Wind directions and speeds at airports are measured at a specific height above ground level. Winds at altitude are typically stronger. Few know this, but as a pilot I do—wind directions will shift depending on altitude. In short, the wind conditions at the WTC cannot be assumed to mirror winds close to ground level several miles away.

It is important to understand where the above recordings were taken in relation to the whole of the North Tower. The 78th floor was the location for the recordings, in my opinion, because the 22-B elevator of interest was an express elevator that had its hoist motor at that level. The WTC towers used a combination of express and local elevators.

But the 78th floor was not at the top of the building. Any motions at that level were interior to the structure, in terms of total building height. The fundamental or first mode would have indicated larger accelerations at the utmost extreme—at the building's top (110th) floor.

Another thing to note is that the above recordings fail to suggest any torsional twisting. It isn't that twisting didn't occur, but rather that a translational measurement located close to the tower's center, presumably also close to the tower's elastic axis, would not reveal any indication of structural twisting. To use phraseology from my doctoral dissertation, such motions were not observable given just those limited measurements.

Chang implied, but almost imperceptibly, that the owners of the WTC in general did not allow the recording of building movements. In my estimation, the reasoning behind the gag order to not allow recordings of movements in the WTC towers was rooted in legal matters as well as economics. As for the legal aspects, no law requires an owner to make or to allow others to make recordings. Also, it was not illegal for a building owner to prohibit measurements.

But if recordings were actually taken, then these can become subject to discovery. Discovery is a legal term or procedure meaning that a court can, and quite routinely will, order that all available information and documents pertaining to a pending litigation be made available to opposing parties in the litigation. Again, if recordings don't exist, the recordings cannot be subject to discovery.

Yet another motivation to not allow recordings has its roots in economics. Reputations and preserving integrity are critical for properties that generate rent. Reports of sway in a building typically aren't embraced by prospective tenants. If possibly damaging rumors or reports were ever to circulate, whether true or not, then potential tenants would be less likely to want to rent space. The simple realities of supply and demand would lower the rental rate, because demand would be less.

As Chang explained to me, the elevator company was under no such restraint or gag order. The elevator company, as a vendor, was at risk. The elevator company had every right to service, repair, and to take measurements on their products. The elevator components, by chance, just happened to be attached to the WTC. Although building owners commonly restricted access to building records, I was hitting the jackpot. Chang provided me with hardcopies of the accelerometer strip chart recordings of the North Tower, taken previously on March 19, 1975. I never signed or agreed to any nondisclosure restrictions, either orally or in writing. As such, I feel free to disclose these recordings as I deem fit.

The recordings provided by Chang were of immense value to me as a researcher, but they also had serious drawbacks. The recordings constituted dirty data. The data were dirty because I had no supporting validation. I had no knowledge or assurances as to calibrations. I lacked knowledge of where within the Sky Lobby or elevator shaft confines the measurements were taken. The exterior wind conditions were only assumed equivalents based on Newark Airport winds being similar to winds impacting the WTC North Tower. Winds near ground level do not reflect winds at altitude. As altitude increases, winds generally increase in magnitude. The wind direction undergoes a shift, as per the Coriolis effect. The turbulence and gust spectrum change with altitude.

Because of these and other dirty details, I was unable to use or show the recordings to anybody as being scientifically validated. I could not use them to refute published claims made by others. I was happy to know the inner tickings and heartbeat of the WTC, dynamically speaking. But because the data would not pass a smell test when and if challenged, I was unable to use that knowledge to my advantage.

As I navigate through life, at times I joke saying that I'm a doctor, but I then quickly add—a doctor of machines. As a doctor with my stethoscope examining patients, my training permits me to diagnose sick patients. The WTC accelerometer recordings indicated a sick patient. The eleven-second first period sway and the beat resonance were ho-hum and to be expected. They were no big deal. What alarmed me was the presence of the relatively noisy and less regular five-second period in the E-W accelerometer recording. I considered it unusual and alarming that something so giant as a 110-story structure equivalent to an acre in footprint and weighing so much could exhibit this symptom. Clearly, I was seeing a patient with hypertension or heart flutter symptoms. The strip chart measurements were taken well within the chest cavity, not at some extreme tip or end. The confused behavior of the E-W accelerations suggested the WTC North Tower was getting bullied.

The bully was obviously gusty winds, vortex shedding, and that the winds were shifting in direction. The accelerometer readings suggested some degree of chaotic behavior. I guessed that sensitive dependence was playing a role. Because the accelerometer recordings were dirty and lacking in wind conditions external to the patient, I was hesitant to carry on pronouncing my diagnosis. I will return to the matter of gleaning information regarding the wellness of the WTC North Tower. Refer to Addendum: The Doctor's Diagnosis.

Now, The Reason for my Invitation

Chang continued to expound on why he had invited me. He explained that on windy days vortex shedding from the World Trade Center towers was hammering a smaller adjacent building at 22 Cortlandt Street in the lower Manhattan financial district. The major tenant there at the time was Dow Jones & Company, publisher of *Barron's* and *The Wall Street Journal.* Litigation in some form was pending and was a concern. Therefore, Chang desired to come up with an affordable remedy to control the unwanted sway in the 22 Cortlandt Street building.

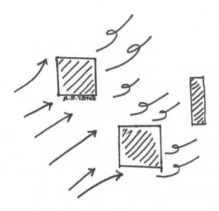

In the above diagram, I sketched the scenario as if one was looking down on it. The two square-shaped towers of the World Trade Center are to the left and lower center. The thinner rectangular building to the right represents 22 Cortlandt Street. On windy days, when the wind was generally from the southwest or west, vortices generated by the World Trade Center towers frontally impacted the smaller structure.

Recall that vortex shedding relates to the trailing eddy formations that alternate from side to side. One eddy forms and then goes downstream from the left side. In succession, another eddy forms and goes down the right side. According to Chang, this downstream eddy flow sometimes dynamically impacted the 22 Cortlandt Street building.

One manifestation of vortex shedding is a cyclical variation in the aerodynamic pressure on the back side of the structure spawning the vortices, as well as on the sides of the building. The cyclical changes in side pressures often cause side-to-side swaying. I assumed that the five-second East-West sway I had seen in the accelerometer recordings of March 19, 1975 was caused by vortex shedding. A second consequence of the vortex shedding was the creation of swirling eddies of downstream air flow at the same periodicity, five seconds.

Unfortunately, the natural period of sway for the 22 Cortlandt Street structure in its E-W direction was about five seconds, which was the same as the natural period of vortex shedding of the World Trade Center. The 22 Cortlandt Street building was narrower in its E-W direction compared to the N-S direction, therefore it was less rigid (more compliant) in the E-W direction and had its greatest frontal area facing the World Trade Center, thus worsening the effect.

Following our initial discussion in his office, our next stop was to inspect the roof of the 22 Cortlandt Street building. As I took in the view from the top of the building, "tower" was indeed an appropriate word for the World Trade Center. Those two enormous giants surpassed everything else. The roof I was standing on was perhaps 30 or 40 stories above the street below. It was awesome to be so high, and yet the World Trade Center towers made the place where I was standing seem trivial. It is hard to describe the exact emotions I felt. Small and insignificant are perhaps good words.

On the roof I noticed the relative absence of wind in my face as I stood looking in the direction of the towers. Because of so much direct frontal area on its broad side, the impacting wind was not horizontal and coming inward at my face but rather directly upward. I stood as close to the building's rooftop edge as I dared. I felt no wind. It was as if I was standing within a protective enclosure. Only when I stretched my hand out in front of me did I feel a tremendous upward rush of air.

In my previous structural work and analysis, I had somehow envisioned placement of any active appendage to be in the vertical orientation, almost like an upward extension of the building. I came to realize that any appendage should, for greater effectiveness, be projected at an outward angle.

At that point and out of the clear blue, Chang asked if any of my proposed control schemes could mitigate the excessive swaying in the 22 Cortlandt Street building. As I sit here at my computer some forty-plus years later, I am still pondering that question. It wasn't some pretend academic scenario sketched onto a classroom blackboard but rather a real-world situation with a real building and real people who were faced with a real problem.

His question was so sudden. I lacked all sorts of information. The circumstance of a building being impacted by vortex shedding had never entered my mind. Another twist was that the impacting frequency coincided with the natural period of building sway.

The scenario I had envisioned and worked with for the past three years was of a lone building standing in what is called Gaussian turbulence (also known as random turbulence or white spectrum noise). The excitation I had previously studied resulted from aerodynamic properties of the white noise spectrum in the Earth's boundary layer. The situation of a structure being pounded by eddies of a predominant (narrow spectrum) frequency that coincided with the natural frequency of sway had not entered my mind.

I still have regrets and second thoughts about that visit. Chang would have perhaps been better served if he had retained my services as a consultant to study the options. That didn't happen. The tone of my exchanges with Chang up to that point was easygoing and informal. Even that day I had traveled to see him at no expense to him or his company. I wasn't compensated for my time, and I didn't ask to be compensated. It was a friendly and cordial visit. The visit was both relaxed and professional in tone.

There were so many new twists and unknowns. I wasn't prepared to jump to a hasty and unsupported conclusion. Also remember that retrofitting a structure after it has been erected involves considerable cost and complexity. In some cases, certain candidate retrofits are no longer viable because the building presents limitations. Once any building is completed and occupied, it becomes extremely costly to make changes. But given the circumstances as explained by Chang, I tried to digest the situation. Short of dismantling the building, I saw two possible retrofit options.

One option was to contemplate the use of aerodynamic sway stabilization. However, if aerodynamic appendage manipulation would have been retroactively invoked, it would have been more appropriate to retrofit active appendages onto the World Trade Center towers rather than 22 Cortlandt Street. My assertion, although untested, is that manipulated smart appendages can be configured to disorganize vortex shedding. Therefore, addressing the source of the vortex shedding could have reduced the sway of the affected building.

The second option was a more traditional solution of beefing up the 22 Cortlandt Street building's structure. The easiest approach would be to add additional bracing using the available access to the elevator shafts.

If my memory hasn't failed me, my recollection is that Chang believed the 22 Cortlandt Street building would undergo retrofitting by installation of additional bracing within its elevator shaft confines. Such a remedy would be logical. Increased structural stiffness would accomplish the critical goal of making the structure stiffer in the E-W direction, thereby shifting the natural swaying to a higher frequency. The problem's root was that the vortex shedding frequency from the World Trade Center and the natural frequency of sway of the impacted building in its E-W direction closely coincided.

Few or even no practical options existed for eliminating the vortex shedding coming from the World Trade Center, but stiffening the 22 Cortlandt Street structure was viable. The elevator shafts could be made accessible without greatly disrupting the building's occupants. The work of installing bracing in elevator shafts could be performed sequentially, one elevator shaft at a time.

I have no knowledge if that retrofit was ever undertaken. I will say that on 9/11, several adjacent buildings to the World Trade Center were destroyed or damaged in the resulting collapse. One such building was 22 Cortlandt Street. It has since been replaced with an entirely new and shorter building.

I Finally See the 3M Dampers

During my visit with Chang, I requested to see firsthand an installed typical 3M damper. Chang graciously agreed. We proceeded from the 22 Cortlandt Street building to our next stop and ascended the South Tower by express elevator. At the 78th floor Sky Lobby, we switched to a local elevator that took us to the 82nd floor. Some upper floors were still undergoing construction, and the interiors were being finished for occupancy. Some of the 3M dampers as well as the structural steel beams were in plain view. I was delighted to at last see the dampers in the real world and to be able to even briefly discuss the dampers with the World Trade Center structural engineers.

The goal of installing dampers was to increase the internal energy dissipation, hence damping, in the towers.

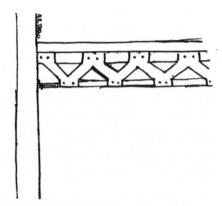

The above figure, which follows Mahmoodi et al [18], illustrates the configuration of a typical 3M damper. Each of the many dampers consisted of two layers of viscous-elastic material sandwiched between two outer steel plates and one center plate.

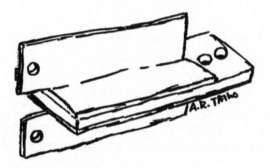

This schematic shows the configuration of a typical damper with the two viscous-elastic layers.

The damper ends were attached to the World Trade Center vertical structural columns and the bottom end of each suspended ceiling truss. Published literature stated that 10,000 viscous-elastic dampers had been installed in each tower, starting on about the 10th and all floors above.

The 3M dampers were attached as follows:

1. The ends of the dampers were pre-drilled to accept bolts.
2. Each damper was attached on one end by bolts to the lower end or vertex of the prefabricated ceiling truss. Holes had to be drilled in the trusses to accept bolts.
3. A pre-drilled angle bracket was attached by welding onto the

vertical support column.

4. The second end of the 3M damper was bolted to the angle attachment bracket.

The entire operation was repeated 20,000 times, so fixtures and procedures were standardized. Drilling was not done in the vertical support columns. Whenever a structural member is drilled, two bad things happen: (1) the cross-sectional area is reduced, and (2) the presence of the drilled hole creates a stress concentration, increasing the stress by a factor of three. Prudent designers will strive to avoid stress concentrations whenever possible, especially if the structural member is critical. Therefore, in my estimation, the installation required the angle support brace to be welded on. This appears to be the most likely attachment method because welding doesn't require access to the reverse side or inside of the structural vertical column, and will preserve the entirety of the supporting column's design strength.

During my inspection tour in 1975, I did not take specific note of how the dampers were attached. The above procedures were inferred based on published documents.

As a person with expertise in mechanical devices and dampers, I was skeptical at the onset and remain skeptical to this day. I considered the 3M dampers inappropriate to the World Trade Center application. The viscous-elastic material will dissipate energy, but only to the extent that the dampers are exercised.

Furthermore, my skepticism was rooted in the application and not in the damper properties. Dampers of this type are based on dissipation of energy as related to hysteresis, but such mathematical discussions are best relegated to engineering classroom lectures. The application to the World Trade Center situation seemed to have missed the target. The central point is that a decision was made post-construction to install 10,000 dampers in each tower. This decision to retrofit in turn significantly impacted the completion date of the World Trade Center.

While my curiosity was satisfied once I had the opportunity to inspect an actual 3M damper installed in the World Trade Center, my well-trained eyes then saw something totally unexpected. I observed that the WTC lacked heat-retarding insulation on the supporting steel structural columns and prefabricated overhead trusses. There was no hint or evidence of any plan to install heat-protective insulation on the structural members.

The fire rating of a structure is determined by how long it will retain its structural integrity when subjected to heat. Skyscrapers of the early days typified by the Chrysler Building (completed 1930) and the Empire

State Building (completed 1931) used steel beams encapsulated with masonry and/or concrete. The concrete and masonry made these earlier buildings both rigid and essentially fireproof. On July 28, 1945, a B-25 Mitchell bomber, lost in foggy conditions, accidentally crashed into the Empire State Building's 79th floor, yet, because of the masonry in the structure and its masonry exterior, the B-25 bomber did minimal damage.

As well as making a structure more fireproof, concrete encapsulation of the structural beams causes the structural damping properties to be greater, resulting in less building sway. In contrast, the newer generation of steel and clad structures is less rigid and more elastic. They are also inherently less well damped.

This may sound contradictory, but even older wooden warehouses with huge wooden beams can be rated as more fireproof than a modern steel and glass-clad structure. This is because when a dimensionally large beam burns, it will char on the outside, sealing the interior from the oxygen supply and insulating it from the heat. Wood has a significantly lower *coefficient of thermal conductivity* as compared to steel. Also, wood does not experience a sharp drop in its strength upon being heated. The wood below the charred level will be relatively cool and will retain up to 90% of its structural integrity. Ferrous metals, notably steel, begin to dramatically weaken upon reaching a critical temperature.

The World Trade Center represented an "advance" in architectural and construction techniques. The former methods of concrete encapsulation of the structural support columns had been eliminated. The height, the generous floor space, and the open areas had reached new limits. The towers each had 110 floors, plus some additional underground floors. The vertical loads were carried by the outer perimeter support columns and the interior columns that formed the core. The rectangular core housed the many elevator shafts, stairwells, and services. The interior floors extending outward from the core to the perimeter were open with no interior load-bearing walls or supports. The longer internal spans between supports permitted tenants to position interior walls or dividers with great flexibility.

But the steel structural beams and overhead trusses had no insulation. Furthermore, Chang informed me that a building code waiver had been granted to eliminate the requirement for application of any heat-insulating protection on all floors above the 20th.

Having a fear of fire traps is a part of my DNA. In my book *We're All Set* [21], I comment on my mother's fear of fire traps. One story concerned how my mother bailed out of a moving car. Upon hearing that the car was on fire, shouted out by a passing motorist, her survival instincts dictated her immediate reaction. The year was about 1948. The family car was a 1941 Dodge four-door sedan. The emergency brake was mounted on a drum at the rear of the transmission. In those days engines and transmissions commonly had poor seals and gaskets. Engine oil and transmission grease had permeated the emergency brake band. My father, who was driving, had forgotten to release the emergency brake. The friction started a fire. The fire was located directly under the center of the car and passenger compartment. Our family of five was merrily riding along, returning from an outing. I'm sure my father had important things on his mind, such as, "What's for supper tonight?" Being summertime, our car windows were all wide open.

Then, the passing motorist loudly shouted out, "Your car is on fire!" My mother's immediate instinct to fend for herself was so embedded in her, she never hesitated a second. She opened her car door, as she was sitting up front, and bailed out. She tumbled on some grass in a shallow roadside ditch. The car's speed at the time was perhaps twenty-five mph. My mother's survival instinct was so strong that she never even thought about the safety of her three children in the back seat. My two older brothers and I were left in a burning car to fend for ourselves. Another twist was that that Dodge sedan had suicide doors. The back doors opened forward. My two brothers and I couldn't have gotten out even if we attempted.

Apparently, the apple doesn't fall far from the tree, as I am keenly sensitized to such risks.

I breathed a deep sigh of relief as I left that death trap on that cold Tuesday afternoon of December 23, 1975.

~~~~

"Grandpa," said Noah, "as I learn more about the World Trade Center and how you use reasoning, I'm also beginning to understand you better. You seem to have so much respect for mathematics and how mathematicians think. It seems that you have come to rely on basic truths. I learned that these are called theorems. It's obvious to me that you have a deep respect for Pontryagin's Maximum Principle. To sum that up, it is preferable to go to extremes—and then do an abrupt switch or reversal. Surely, a day came when you were going full bore forward on structural control research—and then suddenly you did a complete disconnect. That must be when you decided that enough was enough. Your life then turned to a new direction. Grandpa, am I correct? Tell me about that day."

"Yes, Noah," I replied. "There was such a day."

"As I worked for over ten years on structural control, I eventually came to a decision point: I had to somehow get sway data, or give up the ghost. Without documentation that building sway existed, my efforts were pointless. Because I could not legally and ethically enter buildings to take measurements, I contemplated using external cameras. Back then, options like lasers and GPS were not available. Instead, I had cameras and an understanding of optics and magnification. If I placed a stable camera on a sidewalk aimed up, I could use high resolution and magnified images to take a timed sequence of photographs. I planned to use a light attached atop the structure as my primary target. At night, bright stars would act as an invariant background. By use of photography, I could calibrate and record movements over time, although there would be film and development costs, as well as delays in waiting for film to be processed. Another unknown I had to take into account was the reaction of blind reviewers and journal editors to my results. If my approach would be considered as off-the-chart and preposterous, what would be the point? My results could be sound, but considering the climate I faced, was I willing to work so hard just to be dismissed offhand?

"I had to make a decision: either to embark on that path, or to pick up some other research activity. There was no middle ground. It was an all or nothing decision.

"I decided to cut my losses. I would not spend time and money to live in New York City just to take some photographs. I also had strong doubts about the visibility of stars. Stars are not very visible when standing in a large urban area, as the lights coming from the city tend to overpower stars. I could have faced days of overcast and rain. Even if I had a clear night, I couldn't guarantee or even know prevailing wind conditions. On the street at night, I would be subject to mugging, armed criminal action, panhandlers each with their own sob story, and possible arrest. But without sway data, I could not advance. For me, that was my breaking point. That was when I turned to bicycle research."

"I understand," said Noah. "It's sad to think of how awkward it must have been for you, just trying to conduct research and live by the rules. You had virtually no budget, yet you were judged by the standards of people who had access to mammoth resources and budgets. Everybody has a breaking point—the final straw that breaks the camel's back."

How Structural Sway Issues Led to the WTC Collapse

September 11, 2001, 9:59 a.m.: The South Tower of the World Trade Center collapses, fifty-six minutes after the impact of Flight 175. Its destruction is viewed and heard by a vast television and radio audience. As the roar of the collapse goes silent, tremendous gray-white clouds of pulverized concrete and gypsum rush through the streets. Most observers think a new explosion or impact has produced smoke and debris that now obscures the South Tower, but once the wind clears the smoke, it becomes clear that the building is no longer there. [4]

Why Come Forward Now?

I was hesitant for years following 9/11 to make my knowledge public. America was still evaluating and adjusting to post-9/11 reality. Numerous places existed where America was vulnerable. My sense is that in 2019 my story can, at last, be told. I believe that America needs to understand what I saw so that our infrastructure as well as our national resolve can be hardened. Until and unless I see evidence to the contrary, my belief is that the structural beams at the time and point of impact were without heat-insulating foam. Without it, the collapse was a certainty once the fuel-laden airliners impacted the World Trade Center.

The vulnerability of the towers was especially true as the flimsy exterior cladding provided scant protection from such attacks.

The decision for me to tell my story was not an easy one. Enemies of America would benefit if the chinks in our armor were made public. We also need to show respect for the thousands of victims who merely went to work that day. Certainly, litigations for damages have occurred and have been presumably adjudicated. I am not an attorney, so legal questions such as statutes of limitations for redressing grievances are beyond me.

~~~~

Noah took a deep breath and tried to absorb the enormity of the tragedy. "That's terrible, Grandpa," he said. "Because of the Port Authority's desire to save money, and their arrogance in assuming the building was indestructible, they cut corners and are responsible for the deaths of many innocent people."

"That's what I believe, Noah," I said. "I'm basing my conclusions on the knowledge I have about structures and the evidence of my own eyes."

"So why did you decide to come forward now and write this book?" Noah asked. "Do you think people are ready to hear it now?"

Deadly Results of the Waiver

On September 11, 2001, the South Tower proceeded to collapse because of heat-induced structural failure. The collapse happened fifty-six minutes following the impact of the hijacked airliner.

In 2002, the United States Federal Emergency Management Agency (FEMA) issued a post-collapse overview study that discussed various aspects of the World Trade Center design and construction [22]. That study suggested that heat-protective insulation was present. Nevertheless, what I personally viewed on December 23, 1975 conflicted with the cited FEMA report. In "The World Trade Center and 9/11: A Discussion on Some Design Issues, Safe Buildings for This Century," Wilkinson [23] also stated that heat-protective insulation on structural beams was in place on 9/11. I submit that Wilkinson authored his report post-collapse without a firsthand inspection prior to or following the collapse. I assume that Wilkinson relied on other documentation, such as the FEMA report [22], and did not have firsthand knowledge.

Because an obvious contradiction exists, I can only state what I saw to be the case, along with what I was told by the WTC structural engineers at the time. I have learned through my life's experiences, often with considerable pain, that things that get built by others can sometimes deviate from the original specifications. The reasons are varied and even unpredictable. In my mind, it is unquestionable that the architectural firm at the outset of the design specified spray-on insulating foam. I have read reports that in April 1970, the New York City Office of Air Resources ordered the World Trade Center contractor to cease application of asbestos-based insulating foam. The prohibition related to asbestos content, but illustrates the original intention of applying insulating material.

When the authors performed the post-collapse FEMA research on the World Trade Center construction specifications, an early move was obviously to obtain and inspect the architectural drawings and specifications. Unfortunately, changes made along the way, especially in the field or at the point of assembly, do not always get annotated on the original specifications. The question in the end boiled down to establishing whether spray-on insulation was present or not at the respective points of impact on 9/11.

For the record, on December 23, 1975, on approximately the 82nd floor of the South Tower, I saw with my own eyes that all of the vertical structural columns and prefabricated horizontal ceiling trusses were devoid of any form of insulation protection.

The Horse Was out of the Barn

When I toured the World Trade Center in December 1975, the towers were essentially finished and were largely occupied. It would be possible to apply spray-on foam on a floor-by-floor basis as tenants and leases might change, but to go back through the entire structure, bottom to top, would have represented a Herculean and costly task.

Even if Chang realized that he had inadvertently overlooked a detail, the entire project was several years beyond any return. The spraying of heat-protective foam was customarily done as a sequenced step during construction. To retrofit the twin towers with spray-on foam, it would have been necessary to empty each floor and gut it down to the structural beams. Fifty-thousand occupants and their personal items would have to be displaced. Any after-the-fact foam application would entail removal of most or all interior wall paneling and drop ceilings. Access would be required to all perimeter columns, core columns, and ceiling trusses. Excess foam on windows would have to be removed, or such windows would have to be protected during the spray-on application. All flooring would have to be covered or removed and replaced. The time for that step in the World Trade Center project had long passed.

In my mind, the horse had run out of the barn; the genie was out of the bottle. There was no easy way to turn back the clock. Moreover, few people back then ever envisioned that terrorists would fly fuel-laden airliners with passengers directly into a building that stood as a symbol of America.

Sequence of Events Leading to the Collapse

Throughout this book, I've laid the groundwork so that we can now arrive at this point: the summary of my conjectures. It is a gigantic list of sequential events and happenings that plausibly led to the deadly failure.

- A standard practice in tall building design was and is to perform scale model wind tunnel tests. The architects, structural engineers, and wind tunnel experts failed to adequately predict the excessive World Trade Center sway and torsional motion. Wind tunnel tests use rigid models, so prediction of any internal building sway is beyond the present science of wind tunnel testing.

- The World Trade Center excitations were observed only after the towers were framed and clad, around 1968. That is when the need for a retrofit remedy was recognized and sought.

- The idea to retrofit the 3M dampers was conceived as a candidate remedy. The use of viscous-elastic dampers on this scale had never been attempted before. Nonetheless, the 3M Company was contracted to supply said dampers—10,000 in each building, 20,000 in all. To my eye, each damper was approximately three feet in length. The details of the dampers are published and available elsewhere [18]. One source is the U.S. Patent [24] assigned to 3M Company.

- It required time to understand the sway issues and to arrive at specifications, design the solution, procure materials, manufacture, ship, and install 20,000 dampers. The addition of another step in the construction obviously impacted the scheduling of other work as well as the World Trade Center's completion date.

- Because of the proposed plan to mount the dampers on the vertical support columns and truss ends, the operation of spraying on insulating foam was presumably impacted. Moreover, if the spray-on foam had already been in place, the retrofit mounting of the dampers would have been more difficult and costly as the truss ends and adjacent vertical columns would have to be cleaned of insulating foam and any bonding residues. The alternative was to either delay or eliminate the application of foam. The manufacture and installation of the 20,000 dampers took priority.

- The prohibition on asbestos-based insulation was a compounding obstacle.

- Any significant delay in completion of the World Trade Center would strongly impact overall costs. I estimate at least a six-month delay in building completion. Imagine how costly the loss of rents would be. In addition, possible contractual lease penalties would be triggered by any occupancy delay.

- A request for a waiver was made to the governing building code authority to exempt the World Trade Center from the application of spray-on insulating foam. Such a waiver, which was obviously requested and obviously granted, vastly simplified matters and accelerated the estimated completion date.

- I conjecture that the NYFD inspectors did not have jurisdiction. If any sign-off on fire codes was required, again the right hand asked for approval and the left hand complied. I conjecture that the NYFD was under obligation to respond on 9/11, but that its fire inspectors had no prior active role or authorization. Sadly, the death toll included 343 NYFD responders and seventy-one police officers. Those numbers are staggering.

- Because the 3M damper installation was a relatively isolated task of welding in place, drilling, and bolting, other construction tasks could proceed simultaneously. A central goal in any large construction project is to shorten the overall construction time. The underlying reason is related to the *time value of money*. Money invested up front and during construction can't start to generate income until the structure is rented. The determining factors or constraints, when placed in consecutive order, define the project's *critical path*. The waiver's primary purpose, in my estimation, was to substantially shorten the critical path, resulting in a shortened overall construction time. The application of spray-on foam would have required substantial pre- and post-operations, with no other operations occurring in the affected area. Installation of dampers would have had to precede the spraying on of insulation.

- All floors above the 20th floor, according to Chang, had no insulating foam applied on load-bearing columns and ceiling trusses.

- For the dampers to work best, they should *not* be thermally insulated because unwanted building motion would be converted to heat. The heat generated in the damper material would then need to be dissipated.

With the above conjectural scenario stated, here is my opinion regarding the obligation of civil servants and experts. Public officials were and are obligated to oversee and to safeguard the public-at-large, something that was grievously overlooked. In my altruistic mind, I consider such violations of the public trust as scandalous, gross malpractice, and bordering on criminal.

On one hand, the "why" baffles me, but on the other hand, it doesn't. Why would building code commissions, building inspectors, and fire safety inspectors go along with such delusionary thinking? Of course, I do have my suspicions. You can't fix stupid.

Let's be perfectly frank. When somebody designs and erects a structure as colossal as the World Trade Center in downtown Manhattan, hundreds if not thousands of responsible, knowledgeable, and certified persons participate, observe, and know what is going on. Why is it that barely a word has been said about the lack of heat-insulating protective foam on the World Trade Center's structural beams? Is there not a single person grown up enough to stand and say, "I'm sorry. I made a mistake"? It used to be that kindergarten kids were guided to become responsible citizens. I see the entire political culture responsible for the World Trade Center, and they are engaged in a giant CYA (Cover Your Appendage) operation.

September 11 was the day of reckoning. To the best of my knowledge, numerous World Trade Center collapse details have been brushed aside and are not public. These include the building code waiver granted, the architectural specifications, and any hint of corroboration of my testimony.

Numerous commissions and pseudo-experts have performed post-mortem studies and have issued statements on the World Trade Center's collapse. Only God knows what the outcome on 9/11 would have been if the insulating foam had been in place.

One thing is unquestionable. Insulating foam on the support columns and horizontal ceiling trusses would have bought precious time—time for firefighters to respond, time for more occupants and responders to exit to safety, and time for the fires to burn themselves out. My considered opinion, as stated previously, will be restated. If heat-insulating foam, rated equivalent to asbestos-based insulation, the WTC Twin Towers would have retained their structural integrity. Previously, I outlined my reasoning.

In writing my story, I have no sense of what repercussions might come. My prudent side tells me to expect controversy. My story is lengthy. My primary thrust was and is to state emphatically that on December 23, 1975, no protective insulating foam was present on the structural beams, as per my visual inspection. Moreover, I reject any suggestions that heat-insulating spray-on foam was later applied in an ad hoc manner. The later application of insulation after occupancy fails the smell test.

Did I Give up Too Soon?

In keeping with the canons of engineering ethics, I raised my concerns with the appropriate responsible officials and was given every assurance that the World Trade Center was safe for occupancy. I had to respect and rely on their professionalism.

Upon raising my concerns with Chang in particular, I received his five reasons as the justification for the waiver regarding heat-protective foam. I was cognizant of the centuries-old practice in civil engineering to design based on probability or likelihood of loads being applied or not. I disliked what I saw and what I was told, but my distrust of civil engineering is no secret. Whether I trusted civil engineers or not, I wasn't in a position to mount an attack on an entire profession.

Engineers like Chang had passed examinations and were entitled by law to place the initials PE (Professional Engineer) behind their names. I never had any need or motivation to take the PE examination. I have never performed professional work involving public safety. Instead, I was a systems theoretic mathematician. I lacked the legal credentials to challenge the architectural and structural engineering design of the World Trade Center. It would have been a breach of professional ethics for me to issue any form of public statement.

But when fuel-laden Boeing 767 airliners were flown directly into the World Trade Center towers on 9/11, all the arguments given to me on December 23, 1975, regarding their building decisions were proven to be as worthless as fairy tales.

By impacting the towers near the top, the upper blocks of floors fell like gigantic sledge hammers. Those two respective hammers collapsed each of the structures below. The initial collapses at the points of impact were due to overheated structural members failing.

To this day, my conscience still nags at me. Did I acquiesce too soon and give up the fight? What could I have done differently? What should I have done?

The Deadly Gamble

September 11, 2001, 2:39 p.m.: At a press conference, New York Mayor Rudy Giuliani is asked to estimate the number of casualties at the World Trade Center. He replies, "More than any of us can bear." [4]

Were Sky Marshals on the Hijacked Flights?

I have a close friend who retired from the FBI in June of 2001—three months before 9/11. Bill (not his real name) also served as an instructor at the Quantico Marine Base near Washington D.C., where he trained FBI agents in shooting skills. Bill lamented following 9/11 that he wished he could get back into the action again.

Bill then made another remark. He said that in great likelihood, some of the four commandeered airliners on 9/11 had sky marshals on board. Bill told me that they usually sent two sky marshals. The reason for two stemmed from the tactics then in use by hijackers. Recall that prior to 9/11, virtually all hijackers taking over airliners made one demand: "Take me to Cuba." Hijackings were so common that all airline pilots carried the approach plate instructions for landing at Havana International Airport.

The hijackers would board the airplane in multiple numbers. They did not sit together. They usually bought first-class tickets and thus were seated up front. Once airborne, one hijacker would create an incident. The purpose in creating an incident was to cause the sky marshal to reveal himself. Once that happened, a second and/or third hijacker would take out the then-identified sky marshal.

According to Bill, the FBI had a countering strategy. The strategy, again according to Bill, was to not reveal one's presence. Yes, sky marshals were directed to remain passive, to deal later with the situation (such as apprehending the hijackers once the plane was safely landed). Bill acknowledged that sky marshals will never go against stated policies. Sky marshals and FBI agents are highly trained and highly disciplined people. They don't freelance on the spot and break rules at whim.

I lack specifics, but military, police, and even federal law enforcement types are present in society. Based on random numbers, there must have been some military or law-enforcement persons on board those commandeered flights. They didn't act, assuming their presence, because our national mindset was one of non-confrontation. The policy in that environment was to "go along, be passive, and give them what they want." Hopefully, we as a society learned our mistake—and will not repeat that mistake.

The good news is that a sufficient number of good guys aren't restricted by FBI protocols. I assert that airline passengers will never allow a repeat of the 9/11 outcome—assuming that we as citizens retain the memory of September 11, 2001.

~~~~

Noah's been asking some good questions, but I suspect the hard ones are coming up. I'm right.

"Did so many people have to die in the 9/11 attacks on the World Trade Center?" he asked.

I paused for a moment, trying to decide how to respond.

"How many lives could have been saved if the towers had been constructed with fire safety in mind?" he pressed.

"I believe many lives could have been saved. Perhaps hundreds. The towers should not have collapsed at all. They should have stood, even after the impact of the Boeing 767s."

What If?

Regarding my original questions: What if proper heat insulation had been in place on steel structural members as per NYC building code standards? Could the collapse of the World Trade Center towers have been averted? Would lives have been saved?

These questions and their variants have been asked of me numerous times. I will now give my answers. What I say and write does not come easily. We are talking about the lives of hundreds and potentially more people. My response and discussion are based on my best professional judgment. My credentials as well as my many shortcomings have been stated elsewhere. My most glaring shortcoming is that I am not a licensed Professional Engineer. Fortunately, one does not need a PE license in order to have informed opinions. I am stating my opinions after the fact. The public safety cannot be affected by my words.

It will come as no surprise that my opinions will be challenged; challenged by various experts. Some experts have already made their pronouncements, notably in the FEMA post-collapse report of May 2002 [22]. A blue-ribbon panel of experts researched and issued their post-collapse findings. The FEMA 403 report stated:

> "The structural damage sustained by each of the two buildings as a result of the terrorist attacks were massive. The fact that the structures were able to sustain this level of damage and remain

standing for an extended period of time is remarkable and is the reason that most building occupants were able to evacuate safely. Events of this type, resulting in such substantial damage, are generally not considered in building design, and the ability of these structures to successfully withstand such damage is noteworthy." [22, page 2-36]

The above quoted declaration is not based on analysis, but rather is opinion. Words such as "massive," "remarkable," and "noteworthy" are lacking in rigor and are not quantifiable. I consider the above statement as an exercise in self-congratulation and a diversion from answers based on engineering principles and science.

It is said that people who live in glass houses shouldn't throw stones. I acknowledge that in my writing I also use words at times that aren't based on engineering principles and science. I am thinking of words like malpractice, greed, arrogance, and hubris, as examples.

I see a strong difference—a distinction between the FEMA authors and me. I acknowledge at the onset that my writing and conclusions are opinions—my opinions. My post-mortem of the World Trade Center collapse and disaster was not funded by an Act of Congress.

I assert that I toured the South Tower in 1975, after construction and prior to the collapse. In contrast, I conjecture that the FEMA authors never inspected the WTC towers as I did prior to 9/11. I witnessed for myself the absence of heat insulation at the impact point of the South Tower. I did not rely on architectural drawings, as architectural drawings aren't always adhered to.

I have testified that I questioned the WTC structural engineers present on December 23, 1975, as to why the heat insulation was not present as per standard code practice.

I submit that numerous photographs of WTC post-collapse debris support my assertion that no insulation on steel members was present on upper floors. I will also go so far as to say that not a single photograph of WTC Twin Tower debris shows evidence of heat insulation being present in the upper floors.

A follow-up investigation by the National Institute of Standards and Technology (NIST) issued its report in September of 2005 [25]. The findings of the NIST report generally mirrored the earlier FEMA-403 report.

The findings and conclusions in these two cited reports differ strongly from my findings and conclusions. I assert that numerous experts will say that no modern steel-framed structure could have survived the attacks on 9/11. If the WTC Twin Towers were indeed so vulnerable to attack, why then did they get built?

The deeper and unresolved question concerned the standards, notably regarding heat-insulating protection on the structural steel members. The ASCE/FEMA report concluded that the Twin Towers were built in conformity to all applicable standards. The lead structural engineer, Leslie E. Robertson, issued similar reassurances. The obvious implication was that heat-protecting insulation was in place and up to all accepted standards. I have argued to the contrary herein.

On September 11, 2001, many in the world watched as newscasts carried live the respective events and collapses.

We are not talking about some lucky hit or rare fluke or chance event. Two identical buildings both failed and in similar fashion. When two identical structures fail almost identically, the failure mechanisms are not random chance misfortunes. Instead, each collapse followed a specific chain of causal happenings.

In my writing, I take the position that heat insulation was absent at the two respective points of impact and subsequent fires. Given that presumption, the central question comes forth: What outcome would have resulted if code-mandated heat insulation had been present on the affected steel structural members?

I acknowledge that certain lower floors were insulation protected. However, that insulation had no bearing on the 9/11 outcome. The lower floors succumbed due to a collapse and not due to the presence of fire.

The Fall of the Towers

The Twin Towers were virtually identical in architectural design, materials, and construction.

Each of the towers was impacted by a commandeered Boeing 767 airliner. Because each hijacked airliner was diverted from a planned transcontinental flight, at the respective times of impact each airliner was carrying approximately 9,000 U.S. gallons of jet fuel, equivalent to kerosene. Kerosene makes an ideal petroleum-carbon fire accelerant.

I had been told by a WTC structural engineer that sprinkler systems were in place. On my visit on December 23, 1975, I observed sprinklers on the 82nd floor of the South Tower. The unfortunate reality is that water aggravates jet fuel fires. Water is denser than kerosene, thus the kerosene floats on top of water. The fact that one shouldn't throw water on a petroleum-fueled fire was taught to me as a Boy Scout. The water from sprinklers likely aided the spread of the kerosene, thus reaching to stairwells and dispersing across level slab flooring.

The mass of fuel in each airliner at time of impact was approximately 60,000 pounds. This may seem large, but each WTC floor was roughly 43,000 square feet. The impacts affected approximately five floors in each tower. To be conservative, I will assume that the fuel was distributed over three floors in each respective tower. If one does some back-of-the-envelope calculations, the fuel present was about six or seven ounces per square foot, if averaged over three floors in each tower. The mass of fuel was likely less as much of the fuel was consumed in the initial fireball created by each impact.

The stairwells were clustered within the core of each tower. These cores contained elevator shafts, conduits for service, and stairwells. All stairwells in the North Tower were blocked by flames. The occupants above the impact zone had no means of evacuation. All occupants in the North Tower above the impact died. Although fire killed some, a large number of occupants succumbed to smoke inhalation.

The South Tower represented a different situation. Stairwell A, the most northwest in the South Tower, remained passible up until the collapse at 9:59 a.m. The remaining stairwells in the South Tower were engulfed in flames, and thus were not usable. Occupants trapped above the impacted floors were not generally aware that Stairway A in the South Tower was still usable.

Posted and intercom emergency procedures instructed occupants to remain at their locations.

The WTC as office space contained an estimated four pounds of combustibles per square foot. The jet fuel started and spread the fires, but the sustained heat resulted from the burning of contents. Contents in any office environment are difficult to monitor and control. Occupants coming and going tend to carry in and out items such as papers, files, books, a sweater, the framed picture of a cute child, plastics such as ballpoint pens, and countless other items. Over time, the contents tend to accumulate. The potential for contents to burn represents a greater danger than the burning of the structure itself.

Each tower was impacted at an upper floor. In each case, a yet higher block of floors was above the point of impact.

The respective impacts caused fires, concentrated on the impacted floors. The South Tower collapsed at 9:59 a.m., slightly under an hour (56 minutes) following the initial impact by United Airlines Flight 175.

The North Tower, although the first to be impacted, retained its structural integrity longer, collapsing at 10:28 a.m.

The two collapses were essentially independent. The collapse of one did not cause the companion tower to then collapse. Other adjacent structures did succumb, but the WTC Twin Towers each exhibited similar failure mechanisms.

In both cases, the respective blocks of overhead floors fell downward. There was no toppling to one side, as if one side had become weakened such as by the impact of the respective airliners.

The cited ASCE/FEMA report suggested a two-step failure scenario. The report asserted that some structural damage was incurred due to the impact. The second step followed of heat causing steel structural beams to weaken, thus triggering the collapses. If such alleged impact damage was massive (using the word massive as per the FEMA report), the damage would have been concentrated on the impacted face, hence on one side. I discount the importance of the initial structural damage to each tower. If this was a significant factor, two things would have occurred:

1. The blocks of upper floors would have shown evidence of a toppling behavior.
2. The respective collapses would have not been delayed as long. The collapses would have started within a few minutes or even less. In contrast, the collapse of the South Tower was delayed fifty-six minutes and the North Tower collapse took longer yet. Each collapse was initiated at locations subject to sustained fire.

In hindsight, which is often 20/20, the WTC Twin Towers had yet another serious design error. As a cutting-edge advanced design, the floors were designed to have minimal internal load-bearing walls or structural supports. An open-air design would provide a sense of space. The renters could move and reposition interior dividing walls at will. The long expanses created a situation where the integrity of the ceiling trusses was critical. If more internal load-bearing supports had been employed in the design, the crucial role of the ceiling support trusses would have been sharply lessened. The unfortunate combination of long truss expanses and the absence of heat-protective insulation on the trusses was the ultimate folly.

The Port Authority, in conjunction with the structural engineers, took a deadly gamble. They placed a higher value on a quick occupancy and staying within budget—and gambled with the lives of thousands. What was the payoff? The hoped-for payoff was a combination of ego and cost savings. The death toll would have been far greater if the occupants had not voted with their feet. Recall that the Port Authority remained steadfast in its instructions for occupants to return to their respective assigned locations.

I contend that the collapse of each tower was initiated and certain when the horizontal ceiling trusses failed. The sagging concrete slab floors had two effects on the respective adjoining vertical columns:

1. An inward pull was exerted on the affected vertical columns.
2. A localized but substantial moment was applied to the affected vertical support columns. The pinned joints had become constrained and thus able to support a moment. The installation retrofit of the 3M dampers altered the character of the truss-end connections.

The combination of the two added loads on the respective vertical columns caused the affected support columns to buckle inward. Gravity then caused the overhead block of floors to drop, thus imploding the towers as the respective overhead blocks dropped.

After the initial impact into the North Tower, numerous cameras recorded the events that followed. In addition, occupants trapped above the impact zones communicated using cellular telephones. Accurate reports of conditions above the impact zones exist. Camera footage revealed considerable detail concerning the respective collapses and the events that transpired.

The collapse of each tower began when prefabricated ceiling trusses became heated, thus altering the properties of steel and its ability to sustain loading. Structural steel begins to fail at temperatures near 900 degrees F [26]. The purpose of heat insulation on structural steel members is to slow the rise in temperature should a heat source come into play.

From a design perspective, a designed object is defined to have failed when the object no longer meets its original design specifications. As structural steel becomes heated, a temperature is reached where the structural properties of the steel are diminished. When typical structural steel reaches 750 degrees F, the strength is reduced to 86 percent. Upon reaching 930 degrees F, the strength drops to 49 percent. At 1100 degrees F, the remaining strength drops to 28 percent. For common structural steels, failure occurs in the range of about 900 degrees F. For any given structural steel, metallurgists can state the failure temperature with greater specificity. I will refrain from stating specific failure temperatures, but will use 900 degrees F as a ballpark estimate. Certainly, when steel structural members in any tall building reach 1000 degrees F, collapse has occurred or is imminent.

The design and construction of the WTC Twin Towers represented massive engineering undertakings. Reports, such as from FEMA, stated that as many as twelve grades of steel were used [27]. A common grade was ASTM A36, with a yield strength of 36 KSI (thousands of pounds per square inch). Other grades of steel had yield strengths as high as 100 KSI. For example, floor support trusses used a higher grade of steel. For the vertical support columns, at and near ground levels, the thicknesses were larger, thus allowing the columns to support greater overhead loads.

Independent of the grades used, the steel all adhered to one shared trait—upon being heated they became weakened.

The foremost assertion and conclusion in this book is simple. Fires were started by the impacts, as jet fuel burned and spread. Other flammables in the affected impact zones then added fuel and thus heat. The absence of heat insulation on the structural members created a situation where steel temperatures elevated quickly. The weakened structural members thus failed.

I do not have access to the WTC architectural or structural specification of steel used. The specifics of the steel used will not alter or impact significantly any of my conclusions. It suffices that standard quality grades of structural steel were specified and used. It also suffices to understand that the structural steel would exhibit failure upon reaching a critical temperature. In this document I will assume and use 900 degrees F as the approximate temperature at which failure occurs.

My professional expertise is far from perfect, but I assert that the decision to waive heat insulation on the WTC structural members constituted gross malpractice. Most fatalities in the twin towers resulted from a mechanical crushing mechanism (which was the result of overheated structural beams), and not due to fire itself.

Why The Towers Should Not Have Fallen

I conjecture that the World Trade Center Twin Towers would not have collapsed on 9/11 if code-mandated heat insulation would have been in place. Four lines of reasoning support my conjecture:

- A prior fire incident in the WTC North Tower provided strong evidence of the structure's robustness and durability. A serious fire broke out in the North Tower on February 13, 1975. The fire started in an office area on the 11th floor. The fire spread vertically both down and upward via an area for telephone cables. The electrical insulation on the cables was combustible, thus generating heat. The vertical conduit served as a chimney, exacerbating the fire's spread. Sixty-five percent of the 11th floor was engulfed in flames. That portion of the North Tower had heat insulation on its structural beams. No significant structural damages occurred. The heat was intense. Flames erupted out through windows on the east side. The fire lasted three hours. Damages were estimated to be $2 million. Despite intense heat for three hours, all structural beams retained their design load capabilities. Post-fire inspection revealed that all vertical beams and ceiling trusses were sound. No replacements took place. Repairs were made. Life in the WTC North Tower went on.

• Other persons, persons far more qualified than me, concurred with my "remain standing" conjecture. Two of the lead structural engineers responsible for the WTC Twin Towers stated on record that when designed, the towers would withstand impact by a Boeing 707 airliner. The two engineers were Leslie E. Robertson, PE [28], and John B. Skilling, PE [29]. Both men were partners and lead engineers in the firm responsible for the WTC. Both engineers had distinguished careers. Robertson received numerous awards, including two honorary doctorates (Notre Dame University and the University of Western Ontario.) Robertson was inducted into the National Academy of Sciences. In my view, I will not argue that any substantial differences in outcome would have occurred depending on which Boeing airliner struck a particular tower. The Twin Towers were originally designed to withstand airliner impact. The difference came after construction had started. As discussed elsewhere, issues arose which caused a cessation in the application of heat insulation on the steel structural members.

• The combustibles present in the impacted zones were limited. Estimates of four or five pounds of combustibles per square foot can be assumed based on typical office spaces. The jet fuel started the respective fires. As the fuel was consumed, the fires and the heat would have diminished. In the absence of heat insulation on steel structural members, the towers succumbed prematurely.

• Additional time would have allowed firefighters to respond.

I rest my case on the documented fact that the fire of February 13, 1975 was as intense as the fires on September 11, 2001. The February

13, 1975 fire raged for three hours, yet caused no structural damage. Insulation was in place on steel-framing and trusses in the affected areas in the North Tower and provided protection to these components.

It is improbable that I can be proved wrong. Though I cannot prove my conjecture, the incident of February 13, 1975 is telling.

Conclusion

September 11, 2001, 7:00 p.m.: Efforts to locate survivors in the rubble that had been the twin towers continue. Fleets of ambulances are lined up to transport the injured to nearby hospitals, but they stand empty. "Ground Zero," as the site of the World Trade Center collapse becomes known henceforth, is the exclusive domain of New York City's Fire Department and Police Department, despite volunteer steel and construction workers who stand ready to move large quantities of debris quickly. Relatives and friends of victims, many displaying enlarged photographs of the missing printed on home computer printers, have appeared around New York. The New York Armory at Lexington Avenue and 26th Street and Union Square Park at 14th Street and Broadway become centers of vigil. [4]

Can a Leopard Change Its Spots?

My story and testimony are sad for me to tell. I would vastly have preferred to write about good friends, good food, and smiling children. I did not seek out my interaction with the WTC on December 23, 1975. Rather, the WTC structural engineers contacted me. My life has been busy and productive. God has somehow called me.

With this stated, I want to comment on a childhood memory. In eighth grade, I remember teachers using the phrase, "A leopard won't change its spots."

I have little control over civil and structural engineers. I do have control over my life. I can unequivocally state that if I had been asked to sign off on a no-insulation waiver, I would have refused. If pressured, I would have resigned in lieu of such an act. To this day, I still wonder what other buildings the leopards have signed waivers on.

~~~~

"I have one more question," Noah said.

I suspected this might be the toughest question of all.

"Could something like 9/11 happen again?"

I was right. This question was the hardest to answer. Although I'm an optimist by nature, I wonder if we as a society have learned anything from this tragedy.

"I'm afraid it could, Noah," I replied. "But if we vow to always remember 9/11, I believe it will never happen again."

Will We Ever See a Repeat of September 11?

As it relates to the potential for similar airliner hijackings, nobody has bothered to ask me. I'm forward enough to tell you even so. The reality is that such a repeat of September 11, 2001 will never happen so long as our memory of 9/11 remains. The reason is obvious and simple—the passengers aboard airliners will not sit idly by and let the aircraft be taken over. I stand in awe just thinking of Todd Beamer (1968-2001), who uttered the infamous command to his fellow passengers, "Let's roll."

Three of the four hijacked airliners on 9/11 were flown into buildings because our national policy was to give them what they wanted. Only in the case of the fourth airliner, the passengers found out that bad things were happening—because of the use of cell phones which, incidentally, was also against regulations. That fourth hijacked airliner had been delayed prior to takeoff, so time worked in our favor. Passengers used their cell telephones and thus were alerted to the other hijackings and the outcomes. History reflects that Todd Beamer had the courage to say, "Let's roll," to his fellow passengers. During their attempt to regain control of the aircraft from the hijackers, the aircraft lost control and crashed into a field near Shanksville, Pennsylvania, saving the hijackers' intended target and additional victims.

I am pleased to say that there will never be another 9/11 style hijacking as long as the memory of 9/11 lingers, because too many Todd Beamer's will say, "Let's roll."

It is commonly stated that nobody saw the events of 9/11 coming. Such utterances are absurd and self-serving. If nobody saw 9/11 coming, then the Boeing 767 airliners flying into buildings were just random occurrences. The simultaneous hijackings of four airliners were planned events, not random occurrences.

The claim that nobody, even those on our side, foresaw the attacks is patently false. Rather, the problem was a lack of consensus on how to defend America against planned actions of terrorists. As in any large society, different factions advocated differing views as to how the larger society should dictate public policy on terrorism. Defensive proposals such as allowing qualified pilots to be armed had been suggested by some. Such proposals were rejected, and thus prohibited by TSA, FAA, and NTSB decisions. Please don't insist that nobody foresaw the terrorists' attacks of 9/11.

I feel compelled to tell a sad story. In 2001, I met in person a famous war hero, Joseph J. Foss (1915-2003). Joe Foss was the greatest American ace of World War II. He was a U.S. Marine Corps pilot, serving in the Pacific. Joe Foss risked his life daily in combat. He received the Congressional Medal of Honor for his heroism in the fight for Guadalcanal.

My interaction with Joe Foss happened several months before 9/11. He was autographing books at a national meeting. He had flown commercially to that meeting. Like all other passengers, he was screened by TSA. Sadly, the overzealous TSA screener became alarmed by a miniature silver replica of a Colt government pistol that Joe Foss was wearing around his neck. The miniature medallion, about the size of a silver dollar and cast in solid silver, was considered a threat by the grossly inept TSA screener. Joe Foss endured the humiliation of having to remove an award given to him for his service. While in combat in the Pacific, Foss carried a real Colt as part of his flight gear. Joe Foss was kind enough to autograph a book for me, which I shall cherish for as long as I live. America should hang its head in disgrace for how Joe Foss was treated by the TSA.

Book inscription from Joe Foss, an American WWII hero

How Does One Regulate a Dreamer?

Dr. Branny *von* Turkovich, back at the University of Illinois, recommended early on that I refrain from calling myself an engineer. That title is reserved by law for persons who have passed the PE examination. I learned many years ago to label myself with words such as scientist, educator, inventor, theoretician, mathematician, author, corporate founder, holder of three earned degrees in engineering, trained as an engineer, professor, traveling itinerant preacher, raconteur, and even philosopher. The above listed professions as named are not regulated, whereas engineering is a regulated profession.

I was and will remain a dreamer fighting windmills. In my landmark 1972 ASME paper [1], I proposed the stabilization of tall structures by putting manipulated intelligent aerodynamic appendages on them. In today's language, I was proposing an intelligent structure. My proposed remedy was to tame the building by using the very energy available from the errant wind to bring about stabilization. I knew that aerodynamic drag forces could be modulated by making small geometry changes, thus controlling the structure's aerodynamic drag forces based on feedback principles. My doctoral dissertation drove home the importance of sensitive dependence, which is now a mainstay in the mathematics of chaos theory.

As a feedback control systems theorist, I saw the problem of building sway as a candidate for application of feedback control. On land, the building is fixed in place, and the wind moves past the structure. The active appendage control of structures will only work when wind is present, yet that coincides with the sway excitation because tall buildings don't have wind-induced sway issues when the wind conditions are calm. Each method to approach a solution certainly has its advantages and disadvantages. I wanted to enter into a discussion of contrasting the merits of the varied options. Unfortunately, the civil engineering profession wasn't interested in such a discussion.

I have not submitted, nor do I intend to submit, this work to a scholarly society and ask that it be peer-reviewed and published under the society's banner. Because of this distinction, I feel that I am justified in declaring certain personal works and creative ideas as proprietary. Although I say that I have proprietary designs in mind, I do not make unsupported claims as to what the performance would be when and if said designs would ever be implemented. Any performance claims implied are predicated on opinions that I hold.

Despite the claims made in the 1980s by the reviewers critical of my work and their assertions that the skyscraper sway problem was already solved, history now tells a different ending. To the best of my knowledge, both remedies touted in the 1970s and 1980s of innovations for controlling skyscraper sway are no longer marketed. Successful innovations for controlling skyscraper sway should now be standard practice, but they are not. In contrast to building yet taller structures, the current trend is to downsize structures. Even the reincarnation of the World Trade Center post-9/11 bears little resemblance to the two gigantic Twin Towers.

There was no question in my mind that I was up against a collective club that had a closed mindset. The closed club had built walls around itself to keep outsiders and non-members at bay. This applied to both structural control in general, and specifically to fire safety in the World Trade Center. Those responsible for the decision not to require heat-protective insulation on the structural steel columns were functioning as a closed club living within its own self-directed fantasy world. Their motivation and modus operandi were based on five ingredients:

- An assumption, based on probabilistic arguments, that potential adverse loads and/or circumstances would not all be applied or presented simultaneously.
- A preoccupation with setting a new standard for low cost.
- Prioritization of completing the building on schedule versus building it as per the original design specifications. They invented their own new standard to keep their actions within the realm of proper practices.
- They fell into the trap of extrapolating their expertise. They considered themselves to be qualified to make decisions in matters where they were relative novices. For example, they deemed themselves qualified in fire-fighting protocols and practices. By placing the tower safety on sprinklers, they overlooked the fact that water has limited applications—water exacerbates petroleum fueled fires. Another example was that an aerodynamic expert, Dr. Alan G. Davenport, was the impetus for the 3M damper retrofit. Davenport was unqualified to make that design modification decision. Yet another example of overreach was the decision to dispense with heat insulation of steel structural members. This third example brings us back to decisions made about fire protection, best made by fire-fighting experts, not structural engineers.
- The delusion that they were in charge and smarter than anybody

else.

Civil engineering is historically based on safety factors. In engineering, one makes assumptions as to the load on a beam, for example. This load is referred to as the *design load*. Moreover, loads come in different forms, such as snow load, traffic load, dynamic load, and wind load. Dynamic loads caused by marching soldiers are mitigated by having the soldiers break step while crossing over bridges. A foundational principle in civil engineering is to assume that the varied loads will not occur simultaneously. A maximum design load is assumed. Then, to be safe, the civil engineering practice is to increase the load-carrying capacity by a factor referred to as the *safety factor*. The problem is two-fold. The first problem is in determining the anticipated individual loads. The second problem is that occupants, hijackers, overloaded vehicles crossing bridges, and nature don't always respect the posted load limits.

As was demonstrated so abruptly on 9/11, our infrastructure as a society stands at risk. Our bridges, dams, power-generating plants, power transmission lines, water supplies, communication systems, and buildings were designed and built, for the greater part, before we ever imagined terrorism becoming a threat.

The world in the 1970s wasn't ready to design skyscrapers akin to airplanes and probably never will be in my lifetime. Some things are meant to happen while others are not. Concentrations of millions of people on a small block of land causes problems. The tall buildings being constructed using shortcuts will be viewed as colossal mistakes in another century from now.

The Warning Signs Were There

In my life's experiences, two basic observations—with some exceptions—hold true:

- The world has an amazing degree of resilience resulting from redundancy, which tends to stave off disaster.
- The world often provides warnings that bad things are about to happen.

Things made of steel tend to exhibit forgiveness and built-in safety. If some connection or component within a larger structure fails, the adjacent whole of the larger structure often steps in and compensates. Steel components commonly behave this way provided one thing is true:

The steel is cold, hence ductile. Ductility, or malleability, critically depends on steel remaining cold. In addition, an intermediate range of temperature exists as steel loses its strength and ductility. For our purposes, let us assume that steel must not be overheated. Even at 750 degrees F, steel starts to lose its strength. Metallurgically speaking, steel below the austenizing temperature is referred to as cold steel. Steel above that temperature is referred to as hot steel. When steel is hot, its ability to support load is drastically diminished.

Provided that steel remains cold and thus ductile, the capacity for steel structures to distribute load is especially true. When cold steel becomes locally overloaded and localized yielding occurs, its ductileness comes to the rescue. In contrast, brittle materials (such as glass and classroom chalk) will fail catastrophically. Glass that has cracked ceases to carry a load. In the case of cold steel, the components that yield will stretch initially but do not quit. This property is but one reason why steel tends to be so useful as a building material.

Warnings in life are common. Consider the expression, "The squeaky wheel gets the grease." Things that are about to fail tend to talk to us in advance. Bearings that are failing tend to heat. That is why professional drivers perform a post-trip inspection, placing a finger on the wheel-bearing hubs and looking for any that are warm to the touch. The same test after the vehicle has been sitting idle will not give such warning signs. Professionals in all disciplines are trained to be observant, looking for warning signs.

Because of the forgiving nature of cold steel structures, and the usual emergence of warnings, catastrophic failures on a large scale are rare indeed. I submit that when widespread failures have occurred, the components were grossly overloaded and that warnings were there but were not heeded. The professionals failed on two counts: poor initial design and failure to heed warnings.

In the case of the WTC collapses, numerous warnings were there to tell the structural engineers that all was not well. The extensive WTC fire of February 13, 1975 should have served as notice that fires do happen and that heat insulation on steel members is critical. Also, as licensed professional engineers, the structural engineers should have known the fundamental concept of the loss of load-carrying capacity as steel becomes heated. It was stated in BIG PRINT in the rule book. On December 23, 1975, during my inspection tour, I questioned the WTC structural engineers about the absence of heat insulation. The question was raised. The WTC structural engineers clearly had chosen to roll the dice. They failed to recognize the folly of their waiver request. In my opinion, they vastly overestimated the protection afforded by sprinkler systems. Water only works on certain classes of fires. Also, sprinklers require a water supply. Water in ample reserves isn't easy to come by on the 82nd floor of a high-rise building.

On February 26, 1993, a terrorist bombing attack was employed to take down both WTC towers. The terrorists planned that one tower would topple to the side, thus taking down the adjacent tower as the first tower fell. That attack was not successful. Six people died and more than a thousand people were injured. The fact that the WTC was a terrorist target should not have come as a surprise on 9/11.

The redundancy of cold steel shows, in my estimation, that the collapses on 9/11 were exacerbated by gross design and construction errors. Even given blistering attacks, steel should have endured and survived—if it had the advantage of thermal protection.

Life provides ample warnings. Those who choose to ignore warnings are taking unjustified risks. It is hard to admit when a mistake has been made. Nonetheless, in hindsight, it is evident that the WTC Twin Towers stood as a public menace. The decision to pretend that all would be fine was a deadly gamble—a gamble that backfired. Unfortunately, hundreds of innocent and unsuspecting occupants paid the ultimate price. The responsible parties were so immature and shameless that they never owned up to their misconduct, greed, and folly. It is challenging for me to think of any design error and professional misconduct of similar proportions. Some disasters come to mind: the Titanic sinking on April 15, 1912; the Hindenburg disaster on May 6, 1937; the Tacoma Narrows bridge collapse on November 7, 1940; the loss of the USS Thresher on April 10, 1963; and the Johnstown flood of May 31, 1889.

However, all of these disasters pale when compared to the 9/11 WTC collapse.

~~~~

"Grandpa," said Noah, "the story you are telling is sad, astounding, tragic, and also intertwined. It seems so incredibly complex, at least to me. If you can, can you point to just one thing—possibly an error made, a stray cat walking across the street, or even the use of an incorrect bolt—that decided the outcome on 9/11? If we—that is, the good guys—were faced with the intent of hijackers to do us harm?"

"Noah," I said, "that's a tall order. But I'll give it my best shot.

"My doctoral adviser, Dr. R. E. 'Gene' Goodson once gave me some counsel. I was getting ready to take my preliminary qualifying exams. I suspected that a committee member who I would be facing had already determined I was unfit to be a doctoral student. I had by chance overheard him remark, "Klein is not doctoral material." That remark put me on notice to expect a rough time during my oral preliminary exam. The usual format was an oral presentation by the candidate, that was me, of the proposed thesis topic. The person who made the remark was Dr. Robert H. Kohr (1925-1969). I deeply respected Dr. Kohr, but in my written exams he objected to one critical answer of mine. I was correct in my answer, but I'll bypass the details here. My problem was that Kohr was convinced that I had missed the essence of his written question.

"I confided to Goodson that my future looked bleak.

"Goodson replied that in life we should only worry about or keep our focus on things over which we have control. As I had no control over Kohr, it was pointless to worry about him. Goodson admonished me and told me to focus my attention on things over which I did have control—my presentation of my proposed thesis topic. Goodson also told me that he, as my committee chair, would worry about Kohr. I now had two things going in my favor: (1) I was able to explain to Goodson in confidence how I was right and how Kohr had erred in the question he had asked me, and (2) Goodson had ways to trade favors and to resolve issues with Kohr.

"I passed my preliminary exam. That gave me a green light to start work on my dissertation.

"With this background in mind, I will focus on the things or events over which the WTC designers, builders, and owners had some control. I will not go down the path of considering if only the terrorists could have come to love America.

"Through the hazy fog and mire, I see one pivotal event upon which everything else hinged. This was the failure of the WTC designers and experts to foresee and predict the wind-induced sway and vortex shedding. The inability to predict how the WTC Twin Towers wiggled in the wind set up a chain of events. A construction step was added, after construction was well underway. The disruption and change caused a cessation of application of spray-on insulation. Yes, asbestos was also a factor, but substitutes existed, although they were not as well known and certified. In my opinion, the ultimate stoppage in application of insulation was rooted in the need, or better yet—decision—to retrofit 10,000 3M dampers into each tower.

"Economics and the urgency to avoid occupancy delays led to the waiver and the deadly gamble.

"I conjecture that if wind-sway issues had been predicted, then the

WTC towers would have been designed differently. Insulation would have been in place. The towers would have been damaged after the terrorist attack, but still standing. The death toll would have been cut significantly.

"Noah, that is my answer."

"Thanks, Grandpa. I will ponder that," said Noah.

Epilogue

September 11, 2001, 11:30 p.m.: Before going to bed, President Bush enters into his journal: "The Pearl Harbor of the 21st century took place today." [4]

Contrasting Two Professions: Civil Engineering and Adapted Physical Education

After many years of getting nowhere with civil engineers, I turned my attention to other pursuits, notably the study and design of bicycles. Somebody bigger than me, whom I'll call God, saw to it that my bicycle research evolved into a ministry wherein children with disabilities were able to master something so common and yet so elusive: riding a bike.

I feel compelled to expand on how the Adapted Physical Educators (APE) profession welcomed me and my contributions. In the book *As Easy as Riding a Bike* [30], I discuss how I presented in Minneapolis in October 1998 to an audience of Adapted Physical Educators. My subject was how modified bikes can be designed and used to permit children with disabilities to master bike riding [31].

In my presentation before a small audience of about twenty APEs, I expressed my desire to collaborate. During my presentation, I told the audience of how flowers are placed on the ear by maidens in Hawaii. A flower on the right ear serves as a sign of interest and availability. Conversely, a flower behind the left ear sends the opposite sign—I'm already spoken for, or I have other plans. I didn't have a flower with me, but I turned my head indicating a pretend flower on my right ear and my desire to collaborate. As a result of my expressed desire in collaboration, three academics in the Adapted Physical Education profession made contact with me. The initial three were Dr. Patrick DiRocco of the University of Wisconsin at LaCrosse, Dr. David Poretta of Ohio State University, and Dr. Terry Rizzo of California State University at San Bernardino. Perhaps the most passionate and persuasive, based on the Minneapolis presentation, was Dr. Terry Rizzo.

A year or so following my 1998 presentation in Minneapolis, Dr. Rizzo telephoned. He implored me to present in San Diego, California, at a forthcoming APE meeting. As the Program Chair, Dr. Rizzo was recruiting me to be a speaker. I said that I wasn't interested and had other plans, but Dr. Rizzo became passionate. He expressed it this way (paraphrased): "Dr. Klein, Adapted Physical Education is a comparatively young profession. Although you come from an engineering background, you are an APE, one of us whether you realize it or not. You already work with children with special needs and implement and utilize adaptive concepts. We as a young profession need your genetic input—your engineering DNA to strengthen and grow the APE profession." His argument defeated my objections, and I agreed to present at his upcoming meeting [32]. By then I had collaborated with APE researchers at the University of Wisconsin at LaCrosse, so my co-authors accompanied me. I had many other wonderful interactions with the APE profession, which are recounted in my book *As Easy As Riding a Bike*.

In contrast to the overwhelming and well-received enthusiasm as I presented at APE society gatherings, the papers I submitted on structural control concepts were unwelcomed. As I attended civil engineering meetings, I received one cold shoulder after another and was rebuked numerous times. I was *persona non grata*. Over the past four decades only two civil engineers treated me with respect: Fred Chang and Dr. John Reed.

My impression of the civil engineering culture is analogous to dogs, who go around urinating on trees and fire hydrants. The intended message is clear: this is claimed territory, and don't even think about entering. Civil engineers fiercely mark and guard their territory. Outsiders are not welcome.

On the other hand, out of hundreds of APEs with whom I've come into contact I have no recollection of any APE rejecting me as a contributing asset.

I designed and built bicycles that permit children with disabilities to master bike riding—to experience the joy of feeling the wind in their faces. Throughout my many years of effort devoted to structure stabilization, I can't ever recall hearing a single civil engineer say as much as thank you. In contrast, parents of children with disabilities are thankful beyond my ability to express. I experience the warm embraces of mothers who I've never even seen before. Their heartfelt joy comes as a miracle has transpired in front of their eyes: Their son or daughter can now ride a bicycle. In some cases, the parents had tried unsuccessfully for as many as ten years to teach their child how to ride a bike. Through my bike program, the child can learn within a few hours. There is a wide age range of participants in the bike program. One person who mastered bike riding for the first time in his life was seventy-two years young. I could go on and recount countless stories, stories of abounding joy. In Wisconsin a boy, age ten, came to one of our camps. The boy had multiple congenital birth defect issues. One leg stopped at the middle of his thigh. The other leg stopped at mid-calf.

The boy mastered bike riding! I am talking about a conventional bike—not some contraption with lots of side wheels and outriggers. The boy was such an inspiration. After he mastered bike riding, he then turned his attention to assisting and encouraging others. He said to one struggling girl, a girl with a dual diagnosis of autism spectrum disorder and Down syndrome, "Amber, everything is possible so long as you try."

I know that God's hand has been at work as He has blessed the adapted bike program and me personally.

As the innovator and founder of an international adapted bicycling program, iCan Bike, which is currently administered by the national charity iCan Shine, I couldn't be happier. Yes, the world will surely survive without active Kleinian appendages on intelligent buildings, but very few will ever know the difference. In contrast, children with disabilities smile, shine, and do things that were, prior to the bike camps, only the most distant of dreams.

Greek mythology tells of the majestic bird, the Phoenix, that arose from the ashes. I cannot help but realize that as September 11, 2001 unfolded, as the giant towers became but ashes, a bird arose from those very ashes. In the summer of 2001, I started my first pilot bike camps. The two camps were held at Sonoma State University in California and at the University of Wisconsin at LaCrosse. From that infancy where about two dozen children were served, the program has now expanded. Each year the program serves approximately 3,000 children and their families. A majestic bird has indeed taken flight, rising up from the ashes, into the shining sunlight. Consider supporting iCan Shine, Inc., the non-profit that makes that program possible.

I take great personal comfort in the realization that tens of thousands of children, virtually all with disabilities, can and will benefit by being able to master bicycle riding. I am truly thankful for God's stubbornness in prodding me along the way, providing new tasks for me, and even for placing a few civil engineered speed bumps in the paths of such children and me. I have truly enjoyed a blessed life and have hopefully become a blessing to others.

In this book I have included discussion of the merits of active aerodynamic appendages for control of building sway. I admit up front that such ideas and concepts are unlikely to ever see adoption, and certainly not in my lifetime. The discussion was included to explain my historical interests in tall buildings and to demonstrate to the reader the extent of my research and involvement with the civil and structural engineering professions. My purpose was to demonstrate my efforts, not my successes. My concepts have been incorporated in a cutting-edge structure in Japan. I have been credited in the literature for the idea behind the Triton Square complex in Tokyo, Japan [33]. I realize I have few successes to show for my decades of work. However, I am not bitter, but joyful. I never designed something in which thousands perished. If you as reader sense a tone of bitterness, please change that thinking.

The refusal of the civil engineering profession to even consider systems theoretic possibilities gives me ever the more reason to rest comfortably. Hopefully, I will be acknowledged as having tried my utmost, even if I have failed.

As I bring this work on structural control to its end, I still have more to write. I thank you for joining me on this journey, and I hope you will find me on my new journeys.

~~~~

"Grandpa," said Noah. "We've put in a long day. I have other things to attend to, plus get some sleep. I suggest we wrap up our discussion. I must admit that I can tell that you were a professor and good at explaining things. I get the feeling that if you ever decided to open the spigot full bore, well, that would be like trying to drink from a fire hydrant."

I replied, "Noah, it has been my pleasure. I enjoy spending time with you. As men we seldom say these things, but we should more often. I am proud of you, and I love you."

"Gee, Grandpa," said Noah, "I have learned a lot. But come to think of it, there is one detail that we seem to have skipped over. Early on you said something and never came back to it. You said that as a new starting assistant professor, you selected two areas for your research. I can see how structural control was one, but you never mentioned the second—which was the problem of explaining the Earth's periodic ice ages. Are ice ages, ill-behaved wiggly buildings, and bicycles similar? If you can explain ice ages, does that impact another big question—climate change? What do they all possibly have in common?"

I took a deep breath. I looked at Noah and said, "We'll talk about all this, including ice ages, some other day. I will see that we have a large dry erase board, what I call a talking board, and some popcorn. Yes, ice ages, bicycles, and structural control all have things in common. Oh, and about ice ages: I have a reading assignment. Look up a Russian mathematician by the name of A. M. Lyaponov."

Addendum: The Doctor's Diagnosis

My grandson Noah was listening, but I could tell that other thoughts were on his mind. He was doodling on a piece of paper. The doodling seemed random, but I sensed he was formulating a question.

"Noah," I said. "Do you have any questions?"

Noah hesitated, then asked, "Grandpa, way back when we started talking about the World Trade Center, you said you were a doctor of machines and that you were pretty adept at coming up with a diagnosis if a machine was ailing. Then for some reason you cut off the discussion. I think you said you didn't have enough information to proceed with your diagnosis of your patient—the World Trade Center North Tower. You had shown me an accelerometer recording taken by the service people from the elevator company." He pulled a piece of paper from a stack on the table. "I have the accelerometer recordings right here. Let's look at them again. I'm sure there are some clues or tell-tale signs that will shed more light and allow you to make some sort of diagnosis. Just how sick was the World Trade Center's North Tower?"

"Okay," I replied. "Let's take a second look."

"And Grandpa," said Noah, "your doctoral thesis topic looked at how wiggly things can be reverse-solved. You referred to something called 'observability.' That involved taking some measurements and using the measurements to work backwards. Isn't that what we have here?"

"Yes, Noah. We are dealing with an inverse or backwards problem. There are some differences compared to my thesis topic." I then laid out the main differences:

- Our wiggling patient was being impacted by unknown or poorly defined forces. We don't know much about the wind that was causing air pressure fluctuations.
- My guess was that the southeasterly winds first hit the South Tower. The South Tower, which was actually southeast, disrupted the air circulation patterns. It's also a fair guess that vortex shedding spawned by the South Tower was impacting the

North Tower. The North Tower was within the trailing wake of the South Tower. My hunch was that on March 19, 1975, the day the measurements were taken, the patient was getting hammered. It was also likely that the North Tower was generating vortexes on its own. I had to assume that the North Tower's accelerations were the result of several bullies attacking it.

- Nobody asked me to specify where the measurements should be taken. The elevator service people were trying to diagnose an elevator issue. What the larger building was doing or how it was behaving really wasn't their focus.

- I couldn't say precisely where the 22-B elevator was located. I'm getting pretty old now. My eyes can't see things that kids these days can bring up on their smart tablets.

- I didn't have well-defined knowledge of the North Tower's dynamic model. Most of my prior discussion about structural control was focused on getting unwanted sway energy out of the wiggling structure. Accomplishing that didn't require that I know every intricate internal detail. For my structural control purposes, simple models sufficed. My strategy was to use an intelligent finger that would exert a push against the building whenever the building was coming at the finger. Modeling details didn't play a big role and weren't vital to know.

- The question we faced in arriving at a diagnosis was an identification problem, not an observability problem. The identification problem asked a simple question: If we knew what was hitting the building and also how the building reacted, could we say what described the inner workings? Think of the doctor who uses a small mallet and taps a knee. If the patient exhibits a knee-jerk reflex, that means a normal diagnosis. But upon being hit, if the knee-jerk doesn't happen, the doctor knows the patient has a problem—hence the diagnosis. The North Tower was being impacted, but I lacked any specific knowledge of what and when.

"With all those limitations and excuses spelled out, Noah, I'll give a diagnosis my best shot."

At this point in the WTC post-mortem story's telling, three threads had merged. We have now covered: (1) the accelerometer recordings provided to me by Fred Chang; (2) the alleged performance claims cited by Mahmoodi et al [18] concerning 20,000 3M dampers in taming the WTC Twin Towers; and (3) the assertion of Chang that the smaller 22

Cortlandt Street building to the east was being hammered by vortexes spawned by the bigger adjacent WTC Twin Towers. I had expressed my opinion earlier that as a patient, the WTC was ailing and certainly not feeling well. I will now elaborate on the patient's symptoms, the clues at my disposal, and the reasoning that led me to a diagnosis.

The observed symptom that alarmed me was the presence of the E-W five-second vibration, based on recorded accelerometer readings. Here are some significant observations:

- The two accelerometer recordings of the same building, taken simultaneously, were as different as night and day. This demonstrated that each sway direction was its own boss. There was virtually no cross-talk, exchanged sympathy, and what is called dynamic coupling. The isolation of each direction was largely due to symmetry. Each tower had a square footprint with perfect symmetry in its footprint and placement of structural beams. There was no cross-talk because the symmetry created a situation where the mass and elastic axes were collocated on the tower's centerline.

- The five-second periodicity in the E-W direction was clearly associated with movement of some sort. I consider the erratic behavior a telling characteristic. As my reasoning unfolded, the erratic behavior allowed me to arrive at a conclusion as to the motion's source.

- The five-second periodicity movement was indicative of one of two possible motions: either (1) translational E-W motion or (2) torsional or twisting motion. Moreover, any twisting motion would be observable only so long as the measurement location was off-center relative to the elastic (twisting) axis.

- Whatever its origin, the five-second periodicity had a specific source; it must have been either translational or torsional.

- I discounted the possibility of both options acting simultaneously or in combination. In my life's journey, I have learned that nature favors the simple. We as humans tend to overestimate our problems and the adversary. Nature and reality favor simplicity.

- Because the N-S accelerometer record was devoid of a five-second periodicity component, I dismissed the idea of cross-coupling between N-S and E-W translational modes.

- I also discounted the likelihood of a higher translational harmonic in the E-W direction, notably a second harmonic or mode in the E-W direction.

- To this point, I rejected the possibility of a second translational harmonic as the cause based on two arguments: (1) a second harmonic would have generated a relatively clean five-second periodicity without an erratic nature; and (2) the higher (second) harmonic or mode would have had a nodal point somewhat close in height to the 78th floor's measurement location. In contrast, the erratic five-second periodicity appeared to be strong, and not a weakling at or near a nodal point.

- Therefore, I concluded that a translational E-W second harmonic wasn't the source of the observed five-second E-W periodicity.

- Moreover, I discounted arguments that the excited mode was higher, such as 3rd or 4th. I did so because the higher harmonics would have been at yet higher frequencies, thus at shorter periods.

- Fred Chang told me that vortex shedding was being generated by the WTC towers, vortexes spawned at the same five-second frequency.

- Vortex shedding can excite a structure both laterally and torsionally. I discounted lateral excitation based on the arguments above. Vortex shedding at a five-second periodicity would have closely coincided with a second translational harmonic. If that had been the case, the observed five-second periodicity in the E-W measurement would have been less erratic and the recorded accelerations would have been far cleaner and distinct. For illustration purposes, the N-S recordings with the eleven-second period and longer beat resonance were free of confused mumble-jumble. That assured me that the N-S motions were due to excited modes, notably the fundamental or first harmonic.

- This led me to my next conclusion: The recorded five-second periodicity in the E-W direction was due to movement or excitation of a torsional nature.

- Without more knowledge of the torsional modelling, I cannot be certain as to whether a torsional harmonic was excited. However, my understanding and experience suggested that the lower torsional modes, in a structure like the WTC North Tower, were of low frequency. The frequencies, especially the first, would be considerably lower than the first translational harmonic. Torsional oscillation periods would have had natural periods considerably longer in comparison to the eleven-second first harmonic of translational sway. It is reasonable to assume that the torsional modes were not excited. This was an important assumption as other conclusions hinged on this.

- The WTC towers were designed and constructed to be symmetric. Symmetry applied to both directions, N-S and E-W. Because of symmetry, having a square footprint and identical square dimensional shapes going up for all floors, the tower's vertical elastic axis was close to or collocated with the mass axis—both centered in each tower. When a structure is constructed to be symmetric, the mass and elastic axes are centered and collocated.
- The measurement locations were not excessively displaced from the elastic axis—the tower's vertical centerline.
- Therefore, if torsional motions were present, they would have had a diminished effect as seen in the recordings. Locations close to the axis of rotation don't experience as much motion as compared to locations farther away from the twisting axis.
- Just when one thinks an explanation is at hand, one discovers a fly in the ointment: I had assumed that the E-W five-second periodicity was due to torsional rotation, which would have had a possible effect on the N-S accelerations. But there was a possible explanation. A torsional movement would not show up in the N-S measurement if the recording location was situated somewhere on a line, the tower's N-S centerline, that passed through the tower's center, and thus through the elastic axis. If I had access to the WTC blueprints, I could verify this. The South Tower had an open passageway running E-W. The elevator shafts were to the north and south sides. This appeared to be a plausible explanation. The errant elevator was an express elevator. Numerous reasons support that it coincided with the N-S floor-print centerline.
- This reasoning brought me to a startling next conclusion—the jumbled five-second fluctuations were far greater than one would infer at first glance. The five-second period motion was really being tossed about. The reason it appeared to be subdued was illusionary. The North Tower, according to my logic, was being subjected to a strong twisting motion.
- The recordings were taken within the core of the structure. The measurement location was at the 78th floor and was deep within the structure's interior; certainly not near the top or an exterior wall. The accelerations measured at that location would be far

less than experienced elsewhere.

- This led me to my summary conclusion: The recorded five-second period in the E-W direction likely resulted from external aerodynamic forces exerted on the exterior, notably cyclic pressure variations. In essence, the vortex shedding was an unseen bully beating up on the large but defenseless victim—the WTC North Tower.

- As winds varied in direction and magnitude, at different times the buildings were beaten differently.

- I conjecture that this level of external punishment was not foreseen by the structural designers and the wind tunnel experiments.

- Moreover, the WTC Twin Towers were not adequately designed and constructed to take this level of punishment, so the 10,000 3M dampers were retrofitted into each tower to address the problem. The retrofitting of each tower has been documented in published papers, notably Mahmoodi et al [18].

- Unfortunately, the 3M dampers were designed and retrofitted to dissipate or dampen translational swaying. The dampers were ineffective in dissipating energy from the twisting motion of the structures.

Based on the above reasoning, my opinion is that the WTC Twin Towers were not happy campers—they were ailing. I also noted that the accelerometer readings were taken with all 10,000 3M dampers already installed in the North Tower. I assert that the design and positioning of the 3M dampers had little capacity to dampen torsional oscillations.

In my opinion, based on dynamics and the need for structural damping, the towers were poorly designed. The designers and the wind tunnel experts failed to predict the extent of the vortex shedding. Moreover, the design of the towers afforded little resistance to the bullying in the torsional movements. The structures had scant ability to fight back. Torsional damping was all but nonexistent. What torsional damping was present was lacking and not up to the task. The 3M damper remedy was put into place as a retrofit; that remedy fell short. The 3M damper remedy produced five detrimental results or limitations:

1. Even if tests would have been conducted post-retrofit, any tests taken would be for the prevailing wind conditions on that given day. It is unrealistic to assume that every possible wind condition can be tested. The WTC towers, being located in New York City and thereby facing the Atlantic Ocean, could potentially be impacted by a hurricane of deadly magnitude. One can't rely on

a sampling of tests because a potential adverse wind condition was not available for testing.

2. The 3M dampers, as positioned, had virtually no ability to dampen torsional structural motion. Twisting of the structure would produce only scant displacement changes between the relative damper ends.

3. The retrofit of the 3M dampers created a false sense of confidence.

4. The 3M dampers as installed as a retrofit altered the structural properties between the ceiling truss ends and the vertical support columns. I have argued elsewhere in this writing that the presence of the 3M dampers contributed to and hastened the collapses following the impacts on 9/11.

5. As discussed previously, the decision to retrofit the towers with the 3M dampers impacted construction scheduling. Faced with a significant delay, I conjectured that the decision to seek a code waiver became appealing. As a person who likes country western music and the philosophy embedded in lyrics, I am reminded of one song's line: "The girls all get prettier at closing time." What was initially ho-hum and rejected, became pretty good-looking when other options faded away. The request for a code waiver became attractive as closing time approached.

I conjecture that the collapses on 9/11 were hastened by the alteration of the structural interconnections.

"Noah, my esteemed and eldest grandson, that about ends my diagnosis. The patient had congenital birth defects. During and following labor and delivery, the birth defects became evident. The experts then prescribed a remedy, notably the retrofitting of 10,000 dampers in each tower. The towers were indeed massive. The framing and supports were vertical between each floor, going up 110 floors. Each floor was a slab of poured concrete, 208 feet as a square. That represented close to an acre of concrete, an acre for each floor. As a structure in torsion; the mass-moment of inertia for each respective floor was significant. The perimeter vertical support columns had little ability to resist applied twisting loads. Yes, the towers had torsional modes, but these were of long duration, hence low frequency. The E-W accelerometer recording given to me by Fred Chang showed E-W accelerations. My reasoning supports that these accelerations resulted from how the structure reacted to the vortex shedding. The structure's torsional frequencies were well below the frequency dominant in the vortex shedding.

"Note that no building of a similar design will ever be attempted again. The weakness or sickness was not fatal, but instead an annoyance. The structures would have stood for several centuries, if not longer. The collapses were caused by commandeered airliners crashing into each tower. The collapses were certain because the structural engineers knowingly and willfully decided to proceed without application of insulation on the structural members. They had chosen to wager a deadly gamble. Unfortunately, the 2,700 innocents who perished on 9/11 picked up the tab."

Acknowledgements

The author acknowledges and thanks granddaughter Anna R. Tatko for her sketch-work. The author wishes to acknowledge Victoria Lesage, Ellen Meyer, and Bethany N. Webb for meticulous editing in this book and others. Should any errors exist, the responsibility rests solely with the author.

About the Author

Richard E. Klein, by his own admission, is an incurable romantic and altruist. His writings and musings are filled with hope and bright horizons despite having lived through World War II and the Korean War as a child, both of which deeply impacted his worldview. Through his books, he aims to point the way towards a better internal mindset and a better world.

Richard earned his Ph.D. in engineering from Purdue University in 1969 and taught systems theory for three decades at the University of Illinois in Urbana-Champaign before retiring in 1998. He holds a particular interest in bicycle stability and control, and has devoted much of his time and energy to the development of an international program for teaching children with disabilities to master bike riding. Visit iCanBike.org and RainbowTrainers.com for more info.

Richard and his wife of more than 50 years, Marjorie Maxwell Klein, reside in the St. Louis area. They have two children and six grandchildren. Richard writes for them and for generations to come.

We're All Set and *Kisses When I Get Home* are two of Richard's books currently available, and he has many more in various stages of writing and publication.

References

1. Klein, R.E., C. Cusano, and J.J. Stukel, "Investigation of a Method to Stabilize Wind Induced Oscillations in Large Structures," Paper No. 72-WA/AUT-11, ASME Winter Annual Meeting, New York, November 26-30, 1972.
2. Caro, Robert A., *The Power Broker: Robert Moses and the Fall of New York*, Knopf, New York, 1974.
3. Klein, R.E., "The Active Control of Wind Induced Motion in Tall Structures," Paper presented at The Joint Conference of the Analog/Hybrid Computer Education Society and the Midwestern Simulation Council, University of Wisconsin, Madison WI, October 21, 1971.
4. Timeline for the day of the September 11 attacks (last updated 2019, February 9) [Wikipedia].
   <https://en.wikipedia.org/wiki/Timeline_for_the_day_of_the_September_11_attacks>.
5. Kalman, R.E. "On the General Theory of Control Systems," *Proceedings of the First Congress, International Federation of Automatic Control*, Moscow, 1960, published by Butterworths, C.F. Coales, editor, London, pp. 481-492.
6. Klein, R.E., "Distributed System Observability from a Continuum Physics Viewpoint," Ph.D. Dissertation, School of Mechanical Engineering, Purdue University, January 1969.
7. Goodson, R.E. and R.E. Klein, "A Definition and Some Results for Distributed System Observability," *IEEE Transactions on Automatic Control*, Vol. AC-15, No. 2, April 1970, pp. 165-174.
8. Saperstone, S.H. and J.A. Yorke, "Controllability of Linear Oscillatory Systems Using Positive Controls," *S.I.A.M. Journal on Control*, Vol. 9, No. 2, 1971S, pp. 253-262.
9. Gleick, J., *Chaos -- Making a New Science*, Penguin Books, New York, 1987.
10. Cauchon, Dennis, and Moore, Martha Moore (2002, September 2). Desperation forced a horrific decision. *USA Today*.
    <https://usatoday30.usatoday.com/news/sept11/2002-09-02-jumper_x.htm>.
11. Klein, R.E., "Reflections on the Past, Present, and Future of

Feedback Schemes for Wind Induced Vibration Dissipation," *ASCE Structures Congress '91*, Indianapolis IN, April 29, 1991.

12. Williams, D.R. and C.W. Amato, "Unsteady Pulsing of Cylinder Wakes," *Proceedings of the First National Fluid Dynamics Congress*, Cincinnati OH, June 1988.

13. Garland, C.F., "The Normal Modes of Vibration of Beams having Noncollinear Elastic and Mass Axes," *Journal of Applied Mechanics*, Vol. A, 1940, pp. 90-105.

14. Abdul-Rohman, M., "Optimal Control of Tall Buildings by Appendages," *Journal of Structural Engineering, ASCE*, Vol 110 (May), 1984, pp. 937-947.

15. Soong, T.T., *Active Structural Control Theory and Practice*, Longman Scientific & Technical, Essex, England, 1990.

16. Pontryagin, L.S., V. Boltyanskii, R. Gamkrelidze, and E. Mishchenko, *The Mathematical Theory of Optimal Processes*, Interscience Publishers, New York, 1962.

17. IEEE, Special Issue on the Linear-Quadratic-Gaussian Estimation and Control Problem, *IEEE Transaction on Automatic Control*, Vol. AC-16, No. 6, 1971.

18. Mahmoodi, P., L.E. Robertson, M. Yontar, C. Moy, and L. Feld, "Performance of Viscoelastic Dampers in World Trade Center Towers," *Dynamics of Structures, Proceedings of the Structures Congress '87*, ASCE, Orlando FL, August 1987, pp. 632-644.

19. Petersen, N.R., "Design of Large Scale Tuned Mass Dampers," in *Structural Control* (H.H.E. Liepholz, editor), North-Holland Publishing Co., Amsterdam, 1980, pp. 581-596.

20. Pleck, M., L.D. Metz, and T. Conry, "The Use of Decelerative Metal Cutting in the Design of Energy-Management Systems," ASME Paper No. 74-WA/DE-10, 1974.

21. Klein, R.E, *We're All Set, Selected Klein Family Memories*, CreateSpace Publishing, (available on www.amazon.com), 2018.

22. United States Federal Emergency Management Agency (FEMA), FEMA 403, World Trade Center Building Performance Study, 2002.

23. Wilkinson, T., "The World Trade Center and 9/11: A Discussion on Some Design Issues, Safe Buildings for This Century," Australian Institute of Building Surveyors National Conference, 12 – 13 August 2002, Darling Harbour, Sydney, Australia.

24. Caldwell, D.B., C.A. Dahlquist, R.L. Elton, and L.E. Robertson, "Bidirectional Damping Unit," United States Patent #3605953,

May 26, 1969.

25. National Institute of Standards and Technology (NIST), Final Reports from the NIST Investigation of the World Trade Center Disaster, September 2005.

26. *Machinery's Handbook, 27th Edition*, Industrial Press, Inc., New York, 2004.

27. Franco, Michael (2011, September 13). "What grade of steel was used in the World Trade Center?" HowStuffWorks.com. <https://science.howstuffworks.com/engineering/structural/grade-of-steel-used-in-world-trade-center.htm>

28. Alberts, Hana R. (2018, October 13). Twin Towers engineer blamed himself after 9/11. *New York Post.* <https://nypost.com/2018/10/13/twin-towers-engineer-blamed-himself-after-9-11/>.

29. Nalder, Eric (1993, February 27). Twin Towers Engineered to Withstand Jet Collision. *The Seattle Times.* <http://community.seattletimes.nwsource.com/archive/?date=19930227&slug=1687698>.

30. Klein, R.E., *As Easy as Riding a Bike*, Independently Published, in press, to be available from www.amazon.com, pending in 2019.

31. Klein, R. E., "Design and Use of Adapted Training Bicycles for Children with Special Needs," North American Federation of Adapted Physical Activity (NAFAPA) Symposium, Minneapolis MN, October 1998.

32. Klein, R. E., P. DiRocco, B. Oberweiser, M. Mallett, R. Heath, "Adapted Bicycling Taught Using a Camp Format," California Adapted Physical Education Symposium, San Diego CA, October 1999.

33. Christensen, R.E., B.F. Spencer Jr., N. Hori, and K. Seto, "Coupled Building Control Using Accelerator Feedback," *Computer Aided Civil and Infrastructure Engineering*, August 2001.